ANANDA: INDIAN PHILOSOPHY OF ART OF FULFILLMENT

THE LOST SECRET OF HAPPINESS

RUP RANI

To those seeking truth and long-lasting fulfillment over
temporary pleasures.
To the silent watchers, serious thinkers, and spiritual
wanderers,

Contents

Contents

Foreword

"You do not need to travel anywhere—journey within yourself. Enter a mine of rubies and bathe in the splendour of your light."
—Rumi

"Ananda is not found, for it was never lost. It is uncovered, like the sun emerging from behind the clouds."
—Taittiriya Upanishad

Ānanda: verbal noun, literally means bliss or happiness.

Ananda is not merely happiness in the ancient Indian sense. It is far deeper than pleasure, far removed from fleeting moments of joy: Ananda is bliss in its ultimate purity, the unshakeable conviction of quiet contentment that appears only when we are in harmony with ourselves and the universe. Happiness is dependent on events or circumstances outside us; Ananda is independent of gain or loss, success or failure. Only when the veils of illusion fade away, when the mind becomes still, and we awaken to the truth of our being, does this mild illumination remain.

For centuries outside ourselves, we have searched for fulfilment in achievements, possessions, or the approval of others. But the sages of India taught otherwise. They knew that Ananda was not something to attain. Ananda is to remember; it is a part of us hidden under layers of desires, fears, and distractions.

The world urges us to pursue externalities, so wisdom beckons us inward. This book is not a manual for happiness; it is the adventure of the discovery of something that had never been lost.

Ananda is not somewhere else. Ananda has always been here, waiting for you.

Preface

There comes a time in life when we stop and wonder, "What's the point of all this?" We work, succeed, and gain, yet fulfillment is frequently just outside our reach. We pursue ephemeral moments of enjoyment, mistaking them for something deeper, more enduring. But pleasure, as we understand it now, is frequently a mirage—an illusion created by a culture that has forgotten the value of inner calm.

This book is not just about happiness. It's about Ananda, the Indian idea of fulfillment that doesn't fade with time but rather grows with enlightenment. This book, rooted in ancient wisdom yet deeply relevant to current life, uncovers the forgotten skill of living with contentment, clarity, and purpose.

After spending decades delving into the depths of Indian thought—its scriptures, philosophies, and living traditions—I've realized that our civilization's ultimate riches is its ability to direct us within. We have received a spiritual inheritance so profound that it informs not just how to live, but also why we exist. However, in an era of distractions, we have moved away from this knowledge, seeking solutions in outward accomplishments rather than the stillness of our being.

The world today offers promise for happiness on all fronts—success, luxury, achievement—but once duped into attaining these things, one is left with a disquieting sense of emptiness. The more one chases happiness, the farther and fainter it becomes. Ananda was born from this realization.

This book is more than a mere philosophical discursion; it is a journey—the rediscovery of India's lost wisdom on true fulfillment. Ananda analyzes why, in our modern existence, we remain restless despite our pursuits and how this ancient way of living can make deep and steady joy accessible to us.

I did not write this book to present you with another supermarket of quick fixes but a way—one that does not demand anything of you regarding renunciation but rather a shift in your perception. If happiness illusionically has always felt temporary to you, then maybe it is high time that you seek something that transcends it. Perhaps it is time for you to embrace Ananda.

To the reader holding this book, you are about to embark on a journey back to yourself. May you find in these pages the gentle revolution that leads not only to happiness, but also to Ananda—the fulfillment that has never been lost, simply forgotten.

~ Rup Rani

Acknowledgements

Writing **Ananda** has been a journey as much as it has been an offering--deep exploration into wisdom, thought, and inner stillness. This book would not have been possible without the people, experiences, and inspirations that have formed my understanding of fulfilment beyond fleeting happiness.

Above everything else, through the time-worn eras his wings touch, the greatest gift I have received is from the sages of India, those blessed ancient sages, thinkers, and philosophers. These silent and inspirational words of Bhagavad Gita, the Upanishads, and the giants such as Swami Vivekananda and Sri Aurobindo have really also breathed life into me as I have been illuminating my path for these deeper truths. Their wisdom then becomes the heartbeat of this book, reverberating across centuries to remind us of what we have forgotten.

And to my family: thank you for being my foundation. Your love, patience, and unwavering belief in me have been the greatest source of strength. You have taught me, not through words but through actions, that true fulfilment is found in love, presence, and selflessness. Each conversation, every lesson, and every moment of support has played its part in shaping how I see the world.

To my friends and mentors, and to those who have caustically opposed me- thank you. Some of you have been guides who initiated me into life, some are challengers who dare oppose the status quo, and some are just quiet encouragements. All of you in your own ways have helped in making this book. The fused efforts of discussion, debate, and sharing have helped hone my thoughts, deepen understanding, and solidify the conviction that *Ananda's* pursuit is not isolated but a shared journey.

A special acknowledgement to the countless individuals, known and unknown alike, whose struggles, triumphs, and personal quests for meaning have impacted everything I have written. Each of your stories has been an entry in this book from the seeker who questions the purpose of life to the overachiever who finds achievement yet still has a void in it. In your search, I've seen reflections of my own, and in your longing, I've found the urgency to write this.

To readers is why this book exists. Those who have chosen to walk a different path, question the conventional definition of happiness and seek something more profound. This is a conversation between you and me, a journey we undertake together. I hope *Ananda* serves as a gentle reminder that fulfilment is not a destination but a way of being always inside you, waiting to be rediscovered.

In gratitude, I bow to the universe the invisible forces that weave moments, create synchronicities, and bring us exactly what we need at the right time. This book is not mine alone; it is a culmination of all the wisdom, experiences, and people who have touched my life. I present it back to the world with the hope that it brings light, clarity, and the quiet joy of *Ananda* forth into the lives of those who seek it.

- **Rup Rani**

Prologue

In the mountains of Uttarakhand, a monastery stood quiet, and one day therein, I met a man who had nothing—truly nothing. He looked the happiest person I have ever seen; his scant possessions comprised a threadbare robe and a wooden bowl. He lived under the open sky; his routine was as simple as that of the rising and setting sun. And yet when he smiled, the world might have conspired to pour all its joy into that moment.

I asked him, "How is it you are so happy?" expecting him to say something wise and cryptic. He just chuckled lightly and replied, "Because I have not been searching for it."

That was the night that I lay awake in the stone-floored dormitory of the ashram, haunted by his words. It seemed an irony that this, a man who had renounced everything, should have found that which we were all still seeking: happiness, the pursuit of his fellow beings across achievements, relationships, status, and experiences-- all in an extensive lifetime.

Happiness might not be a pursuit, perhaps, but what happens when we stop chasing? Wouldn't we irrefutably assume happiness arises from that wanting less away from the chase?

The Chase That Never Ends

We truly live in a world obsessed with a happiness paradigm-these self-help books advertise for you to learn their "secrets" to that ideal life, there's much too much illusion peddled in ads making us believe that we're just one purchase away from bliss, and social media curates every moment, perfecting them, to help us maintain the illusion that every other person has figured out life-except us.

But if happiness is simply a matter of applying oneself, shouldn't we all be shining in it by now?

More than this, we are conditioned to run about happiness like a dog chasing its tail, hardly catching it. When we think that we have finally achieved what we want, it is for just a moment before we go on to crave something else. It is called the hedonic treadmill: no matter how much we achieve; we end up adapting and wanting even more.

Ancient Indian philosophy speaks of something far beyond happiness, that is, a state called, Ananda.

Happiness Vs Ananda: The Difference We Have Forgotten

Most of us have been raised in the belief that happiness is the ultimate goal in life. Happiness (Sukha), however, is both fleeting and conditional, dependent on some outside thing going right; you are happy if you get a compliment, win something, or when things go according to your plan. What happens when they do not go your way?

Ananda is not an emotion, however, but rather a state of being. In outside circumstances, it leaves an inner steadiness, a deep sense of fulfilment that is untouched by life's ups and downs.

Imagine two people standing by the ocean so you can differentiate. One was holding a cup and waiting for the waves to fill in, while the other dove deep into the water and was completely covered. Happiness is like a cup, always depending on something outside to fill it for existence. But Ananda is like the ocean itself, ever-present, limitless.

But if this fulfilment were indeed more profound than that, what is the modern world undergoing in its seeking?

How We Forgot About Ananda

Somewhere in that rush of progress, we mistook pleasure for joy, productivity for meaning and success for fulfilment.

Distraction, yes; deep satisfaction is rare. Inwardly unsettled, but still enjoying the endless new experiences coming our way. Consume more than ever before food, entertainment, and information yet remain undernourished spiritually.

What ancient Indian wisdom decrees is that fulfillment isn't piling on more to life, but removing the blocks to its attainment. Just like a sculptor chisels away the excess stone to reveal a masterpiece, Ananda comes when we let go of the false ideas that keep chasing happiness in the wrong places.

The Four Barriers to Fulfillment

"Usually, if one looks, one would find that most people are trapped in one or more of these common illusions:

1. **The Illusion of More** – A belief that says: "This one more achievement, possession, or experience is finally going to make me happy," or the attainment of this will keep one going around in circles, reaching for it endlessly.

2. **The Illusion of Control** – That is, just as we can bend life just so, we want it to unfold. Life's real truth is to allow uncertainty to be.

3. **The Illusion of Permanence** – Life does not come with happiness alone-it is temporary. We hang on to those good times, despite fearing them, rebuffing life's rhythm.

4. **The Illusion of Identity** – A lie that tells us we are nothing but our thoughts, titles, successes, and failures. This limited vision keeps us from touching the deeper, unchanging essence within.

Breaking those illusions is what will lead most of us back to Ananda.

Ananda is Not Just for Monks

At this point you might be wondering: is such philosophy confined only to priests and monks?

No, indeed. Ananda lives in the real world. You do not need to withdraw from the humdrum of pedestrian life by retreating to the Himalayas or none of your desires will ever be realized to have Ananda. It can be attained by any entrepreneur, student, parent, or artist fully engaged in life and very much cultivating deep inner surety.

What you experience, not what you achieve, is the secret.

This isn't to deny ambition or pleasure; it is learning to go beyond them: how to live with purpose without stress, love without attachment, and act without desperation. It will be about determining the fine line between effort and surrender, passion and peace.

How Will This Book Help You

This book is not your usual self-help book, nor does it preach a rigid philosophy at any point in time. It is a conversation-a journey we'll take together, through stories and ancient wisdom as well as psychological insight:

Why most of what we learned about happiness is wrong?

How to find the deepest, most fulfilling treasure without cutting you lose from modern life.

The forgotten Indian principles that help grow lasting joy.

Align your mind, body, and spirit towards effortless well-being.

Practical means of applying Ananda in everyday life.

You would not need to believe in its doctrines blindly. This is the only invitation: read with an open mind and apply the ideas to your experiment and cautions.

As you move through these pages, you may begin to notice something subtle yet powerful: **happiness is not something to be chased—it is something that arises when you stop chasing.**

And perhaps, just perhaps, you will realize that **Ananda was never lost. It was always within you, waiting to be remembered.**

The Illusion of Happiness

ONE

THE CHASE THAT NEVER ENDS

In a temple courtyard of Varanasi, I once sat next to an old scholar, who had spent a whole life studying the Upanishads. As we watched the endless flow of the river Ganga, I asked him a simple question, "Why does happiness never last, no matter how much we achieve?"

He smiled, with a face lined with the wisdom of years, "Because you are trying to hold water in your hands." He made a cup of his palms and let the water slip through his fingers. "The more you hold, the faster it goes away."

And this is the nature of happiness—the very definition of it: always going, always just out of reach. We live in a world obsessed with the promise of happiness. Advertisers say that this object, once purchased, will bring happiness. Self-help gurus speak of life-altering habits. Social media persuades us that these other lucky individuals are leaving perfect lives—a life that could have been ours had we only worked more, travelled more, or looked better.

And there lies a problem. Happiness, by our definition, by its very nature, can never be enough.

The Illusions of Happiness

We are brainwashed since childhood to pursue happiness like a trophy: a thing to win, possess, and flaunt.

It goes like this: Good grades equal happiness. The perfect partner equals happiness. The dream job equals happiness. Just set a figure for how much money, and happiness will be mine.

And for a moment, we do feel happy. The great highs of achieving something, the newness of falling in love, and the sweet charm of the long-awaited bliss—these bring happiness. But then something happens. The feeling dies down. The excitement begins to go away, and soon we find ourselves in search of the next milestone, the next goal, the next achievement.

What psychologists refer to as the hedonic treadmill is the tendency of us humans to return to a baseline level of happiness no matter how much we accomplish. Yet Indian sages understood this much earlier and long before modern sciences became aware of it. As described in the Bhagavad Gita, this cycle is as knowledgeable as Trishna—an insatiable thirst. The more we drink, the thirstier we become.

But if happiness always fades, is there something deeper which does not?

<u>Difference Between Sukha and Ananda</u>

Indian philosophy makes a very profound distinction between two types of joy: Sukha and Ananda.

• Sukha is pleasure from the external. It is happiness from good food, achievement, relationships, and sensory pleasure. It is real but temporary—Sukha comes and goes, like ocean waves.

• Ananda, the opposite, is the state that is not affected by external circumstances. Happiness remains as deep, unshaken fulfilment when life tends to be up and down. Ananda is what sages and mystics speak of, not in some abstract sense but as an experience that is present for all.

The Taittiriya Upanishad describes Ananda as the ultimate in existence: more than pleasure, more than knowledge, more than power. It is that unwavering inner joy heightened when there is harmony with existence.

Why Do We Find Achieving Ananda So Hard

If Ananda is our natural state, why do so few people experience it?

For the simple reason that we have been trained to look in the wrong places.

1. We mistake pleasure for fulfilment. The whole of modern life is based upon pleasure: fast food, entertainment, instant gratification. But pleasure is transient. It gives us a high, then crashes down, leaving us high and dry and craving some more.

2. We fear stillness. True fulfilment comes by way of silence and reflection; however, we kill every moment with distractions: social media, notifications, and endless entertainment.

3. Our happiness is attached to the outcome. We say, "I will be happy when..." But that puts joy on hold pretty much indefinitely.

4. We resist what is. When life comes to us, we fight against it. We want things to be different, and this creates suffering.

The Science of Contentment

As Indian philosophy speaks of Ananda, modern psychology has an equivalent: eudaimonic happiness. Unlike hedonic pleasure, which is all about gratification, eudaimonic happiness is about meaning, purpose, and deep inner welfare. Studies show that those who manage to cultivate eudaimonia through their activities—mindfulness, self-awareness, and the development of meaningful relationships—are much happier in the long run than those who pursue pleasure alone.

In one landmark study, researchers followed lottery winners and paraplegics. One year after winning the lottery, most winners were no happier than before. Meanwhile, many paraplegics report finding a deeper sense of purpose and fulfilment despite their condition. This corroborates what Indian wisdom has always taught about true joy rising from within, regardless of outside happenings.

How to Get Off the Hedonic Treadmill

If happiness always fades, then what can we do? How do we exit this relentless treadmill chasing after happiness? The answer will not lie in negation but in redesigning the experience of living.

1. From Chasing Happiness to Allowing Happiness

Rather than run after happiness, start paying attention to moments of joy around you: sunshine on your face, a smile from a loved one, the pleasant feeling of simply breathing. Happiness does not exist; a lot of the time, it is simply ignored.

2. Don't let yourself be Caught Up in Outcomes

The Bhagavad Gita speaks of Nishkama Karma, or, acting without being attached to results. That is doing your best but not tying your joy to the outcomes. When you let go of expectations, you free yourself from constant disappointment.

3. Make Room for Stillness

If you are always filling your mind with noise, you will never hear the whispers of inner peace. Meditation, deep breathing, and even simple moments of silence can reconnect us with Ananda.

4. Reassess Your Definition of Success

What does fulfilment mean to you? Is it about accomplishments or the way you feel inside? Shift your definition from external success to inner well-being.

<u>Final Thought: The Answer Was Never Outside</u>

A Zen story tells of a man who was looking for his lost keys under a streetlight. A passerby asked him, "Where did you lose them?" The man replied, "Inside my house." "Then why are you looking here?" said the passerby. "Because the light is better here," said the man.

This is how we search for happiness—outward, it seems easier this way. But the truth is, the fulfilment we seek has always been there from within.

In other words, Ananda cannot be acquired; it can only be remembered. And the moment of your complete stop becomes the moment of your realization that it was never lost in the first place.

TWO
PLEASURE VS. FULFILLMENT

An ancient story in the Upanishads depicts a scene with a charioteer and his restive horses. The charioteer is our intellect; the restless horses represent the senses that constantly pull us toward sights, sounds, tastes, and experiences promising joy yet often leaving us empty. Pleasure, thus, excites but fails to sustain.

We live in an age where pleasure not only exists but is also aggressively marketed. Swipe, scroll, click—there's immediate gratification awaiting us from all corners. But what happens when the thrill fades? Why does the chase remain endless? The answer lies in our gross misunderstanding of happiness.

Pleasure is Immediate, Fulfillment Lasts

To identify the difference between eating your favorite dessert and watching a child take his first steps. Dessert is a sensory delight—an explosion of taste, a fleeting moment of indulgence. The latter is something deeper, a quiet lingering joy that goes on long after the moment has passed.

Pleasure relates to the senses; it is external, momentary, and often conditioned by circumstances. On the contrary, fulfilment, or Ananda as the ancient Indian scriptures term it, is internal, stable, and independent of transient highs. One is a spark kindling brief satisfaction; the other is a fire warming the soul with deep satisfaction.

The Science of Why Pleasure Doesn't Last

Modern neuroscience underscores what Indian wisdom has known for centuries: there are almost inherent components of the human brain, hedonic adaptation, which readapt to baseline happiness whenever pleasures are interfaced with.

Think about the first time you bought something expensive new phone! Or a fancy car! Or that luxury item! The excitement would last a few days, maybe an ecstatic week. But pretty soon you would settle back into acceptance and begin craving for the next one. This is the deceptive thing about pleasure: It always demands something more.

Fulfillment is not about piling up positive experiences; it is about aligning with what is meaningful. This is how sages in the Himalayas, who have very little stuff, can often express such a profound peace-the kind of peace that eludes billionaires with private jets.

The Bhagavad Gita on Happiness that Doesn't Fade

In the Bhagavad Gita, Krishna speaks of two types of happiness.

1. That which causes pain (Sukha) – it comes from the senses, even one might say from the senses of perception. It depends on something outside oneself. It is pleasurable but transient.

2. **Fulfillment (Ananda)** – a happiness that arises from inner steadiness and wisdom. It remains calm but is

unshakable.

At this point, the act of attraction may lead to repulsion or suffering, signaling a state of dependence on the outside world. This suggests that inner culture is the superior path to creating happiness based on an inner posture.

A great part of our modern culture finds reasons why the two are confused.

For centuries Indian philosophy considered development in terms of the contentment of one's spirit rather than consumption. Today the world has reinforced an antithesis:

• Happiness comes with purchase.

• More is always better.

• If we don't have enough, we are incomplete.

This sort of illusion keeps people on an endless pursuit. But the wisdom from the past tells a very different story: fulfilment is not about having more, but less.

Practical Steps: Parting Ways with the Pleasure Principle

So how do we start putting this wisdom to work in everyday life?

1. **Practice Delayed Gratification**: Rather than chasing immediate pleasure, ask, Will doing this bring me joy a month from now? If not, reconsider.

2. **Detach from External Validation**: Its fiber is true empowerment and fulfilment obtained from within when your happiness depends largely on the approval of others.

3. **Seek Meaning Rather Than Stimulation**: Invest time scrolling that feeds your mind and soul, i.e., reading, creating, or meditating.

4. **Cultivate Silence**: The more silenced your mind becomes, the clearer the vision of what brings true happiness is.

<u>Understanding the Difference is the First Step to Ananda</u>

This choice is simple yet profound- live for the temporary high, or cultivate a joy that abides. While in pursuit of pleasure, one must note: that fulfillment is often mistaken for it. The true definition of Ananda is, therefore, the way out of the hedonic treadmill, to rediscover the quiet enduring joy that was within you, all along.

THREE

THE STORIES WE INHERIT – HOW CULTURE SHAPES OUR DEFINITIONS OF JOY

In a quaint village in Tamil Nadu, an elderly woman once narrated a story, which had been passed down through many generations, of a prince who had everything—wealth, power, and pleasure—and yet was melancholic. One day, he came across a sage who handed him an ordinary clay bowl and said, "If you can fill this with happiness, you will never suffer again." The prince traversed many countries acquiring gold, jewels, and fine foods, yet the bowl remained empty. He came to the sage in despair and asked, "What am I missing?" The sage smiled and whispered, "You are trying to pour happiness into something that cannot hold it."

This is what defines the culture-bound inheritance of our understanding of joy. We are handed a cultural script about what happiness should consist of and we abide by it. Teachings tell us that success, love, wealth, or fame will bring fulfilment. But what if the very blueprint is flawed?

Cultural Conditioning: The Unseen Hand that Forms Our Desires

We inherit stories from the moment we are born. Those stories dictate what we should aim for, what we should avoid, and what constitutes a 'good life.' But how often do we stop to ask: Whose definition of happiness am I following?

1. **The Myth of the Ideal Life**

Each culture conjures an image of the 'perfect' life. In the West, it may be the white-picket-fence dream with some stable job, a big house, and a happy family; in India, it may be anything from a high-paying career to marriage, to attaining social respect. But these are not universal truths; they are constructs of culture.

Take the ancient Indian concept of the Purushottam-Dharma (duty), Artha (wealth), Kama(pleasure), and Moksha (liberation). Contrary to current perspectives of success, which exalt wealth and status, the Purushottam acknowledge that fulfilment is multi-dimensional. Indeed, a life lived only for Artha and Kama, without Dharma and Moksha, is perceived to be an incomplete one.

In the modern context, however, how many people would rather consider happiness as inner harmony rather than some bank balance? How often do we engage in a cycle of chasing success at the stake of meaning?

2. **Role of Media and Society**

Media also plays a huge part in shaping our perception of happiness and its standards in society. Movies, advertisements, and social media portray visions of happiness that are often unattainable and sometimes simply fictitious. We are comparing the glamorous highlight reels with our mundane daily life.

In ancient India, there was never any logic of comparison in attaining the realization of life. The sages, Patanjali, and the like emphasized being self-aware and mastering the inner self. Today, however, self-worth seems to correlate with social validation; the moment we tie happiness to external validation, we are prisoners of opinion.

Indian View: Ananda Over Illusion

In Indian traditions, happiness is never seen as a goal but rather a byproduct of right living. The central message of the Bhagavad Gita is that happiness is not to be found in what you achieve, but in how you experience life. Unlike Western paradigms, which often equate success with material gain, Indian wisdom encourages detachment from external outcomes and being true to one's inner nature.

1. **The Role of Samskaras**

In Vedanta, it is believed that every single experience leaves a mark on the mind, called samskaras, imprinting desires and choices. If someone is raised in a culture where wealth is glorified, then to that person, happiness is naturally associated with money. If someone else is brought up in a monastery, he/she will recognize simplicity with joy.

Thus, the route to liberation from conditioned happiness would be to bring into awareness one's samskaras and inquire about their authenticity. Are my desires mine, or are they an inheritance?

2. **Lessons from the Ragamuffin Path**

Yoga is not merely about physical postures; it is a science of inner fulfilment. The Yoga Sutras of Patanjali describe a state called Santosh or contentment, which is the ability to feel whole, regardless of one's circumstances. This is in stark contrast to the modern pursuit of 'happiness,' which is all too often contingent.

Santosh is something we can attempt to cultivate only through disentangling joy from the outcome and grounding ourselves in enjoyment in the now. Happiness should neither be an award nor a badge of honor, but a way of living.

Breaking Free: How to Redefine Your Joy

The first step to liberation is the understanding of how external forces collectively shape our idea of happiness. This is followed by the conscious and purposeful process of reshaping it into one that aligns with our truth. This is how:

1. **Belief Audit**

Ask yourself: Where did my definition of happiness originate? From family? Society? Media? Identify which beliefs help you and which hold you back.

2. **From Achievement to Experience**

Instead of linking happiness to goals, aim at the quality of your momentary experience. How much are you in touch with your present moment? How much do you engage deeply with life?

3. **Joy with Intention**

Happiness is not something we pursue; it is something we notice. Take a moment each day to appreciate the little things—a sunset, a deep breath, a quiet moment of gratitude. Happiness tends to lie in the conidia.

Choosing Ananda Over Illusion

Because the prince was looking in the wrong direction to fill his bowl, he never filled it. The secret lies no longer in acquisition, but in the realization that there is no vessel for joy apart from living it.

The moment we stop running after some mirage of happiness manufactured by society and set out to carve one on our terms is the first step towards Ananda. This path does not mean rejecting pleasure; rather, it entails consistently choosing fulfilment over illusion, presence over projection, and inner wholeness over external validation.

And perhaps therein lies the real first glimpse of what joy was intended to be.

FOUR
WHY SUCCESS AND ACHIEVEMENT FEEL EMPTY

In the bustling cosmopolitan of Mumbai, a 45-year-old CEO sat alone in an apartment overlooking the sea. He possessed everything necessary for success according to the social yardstick: wealth, accolades, and power. Yet he remained inexplicably aware of a sense of hollowing. Strange emptiness enchanted him despite having everything he had once pictured. Why does success seem empty when, at long last, it is attained?

The Illusion of Success

We're taught almost from the time we're born that success is the goal above all else. The education systems and societal structure and norms are all based on this belief—work hard and achieve more, and you will be happy. But if this were the case, why do so many of the ones who "make it" still walk around with this empty feeling inside?

Success in ancient times in India was not merely mapped against external milestones, it was happiness (Ananda) that was given primacy. The sages understood that basically, our achievements are short-lived, while the bliss that comes from inner contentment is everlasting. We, however, have designed a system to worship the temporary while overlooking the eternal.

The Science Behind the Emptiness

Modern psychology refers to this as the arrival fallacy: the idea that once we reach some milestone, at last, we will be happy. But the moment we reach it, the mind adapts to that new situation, sets a new target, and the pursuit continues ad infinitum.

Take, for instance, the case of lottery winners. Studies have shown that their levels of life satisfaction return to baseline within one year after a lot of initial happiness. The same pattern is observable in people who achieve fame, gather wealth, and get promoted. Success gives a few moments of joy, but not a deep, lasting one.

The Indian Perspective: Redefining Success

An entirely different viewpoint comes from Indian philosophy. The Bhagavad Gita maintains that action (karma) must not be guided by a desire for reward, but rather for an inner purpose.

Krishna said to Arjuna:

"You have a right to your actions, but never to the fruits of those actions."

This teaching forms the basis for Nishkama Karma—doing one's duties without concerning oneself with the results. By dissociating self-worth from results, we free ourselves from the clutches of everlasting craving and disappointment.

The Four Traps of Achievement

In understanding why success is often viewed as hollow, one must look at what traps we get ourselves into:

1. The Trap of Comparison

Success is measured, most of the time, relatively. No matter how much one achieves, there is always someone doing better. This maintains a constant feeling of inadequacy and unrest within us.

Ancient Indian wisdom teaches Swadharma—stick to the path you come in alignment with. True fulfillment does not come from outshining others; it comes from staying true to one's unique nature.

2. The Trap of Perpetual Striving

The modern world glorifies the hustle-more work-more hours-more sacrifice. But at what cost?

The Upanishads describe Shanti (inner peace) as the true achievement rather than material one. We are human beings, not human doings.

3. The Trap of External Validation

Many seek success not for themselves, but for validation from society. Yet, external approval is fickle. Applause today can turn into tirade tomorrow.

Indian philosophy has its teaching of Atmabodha-being aware of self. When one ceases to seek validation from the outside world, one regains one's inner equilibrium.

4. The Trap of Temporary Highs

Success may create a temporary dopamine rush, but dopamine along with all kinds of chemical highs wears off. And then, what remains?

The sages knew: real joy is Santosha-contentment right where you are instead of chasing with a thousand wants.

Escaping the Illusion: A New Approach to Fulfillment

Success and achievement are not bad; it is the soul and deeper purpose with which they should align. Here is how:

1. **Shift from Achievement to Contribution**— Instead of asking What can I gain? Ask How can I serve? The most fulfilled people are often the ones who give the most.

2. **Detach from the outcome**—Work with passion, but do not tie your happiness to results. This will free you from anxiety and disappointment.

3. **Prioritize inner growth**—Material success should not come at the cost of emotional and spiritual well-being. Balance is essential.

4. **Redefine wealth**—True wealth is not in possessions but in inner peace and meaningful relationships.

<u>The Success That Lasts</u>

The CEO in Mumbai had everything other than fulfilment. He was living society's definition of success, not his own. In aligning with his deeper values, he finally found what he had been looking for all along—not only success but joy.

Indian wisdom asserts that without Ananda, success remains barren. The very essence of success is being able to remain cheerful irrespective of reaching the goal.

And that is the kind of success that never feels empty.

The Art of Ananda

FIVE

STILLNESS AND THE POWER OF AN UNSHAKEN MIND

An ancient saying from India reads, "When the water is still, the moon reflects perfectly." But in today's world, our minds are anything but still. It is an onslaught of distractions, demands, and the constant pull of digital noise. Rarely do we feel true clarity, peace, or fulfilment amidst this din.

What if stillness were not conceived as merely an absence of movement? What if it were an exalted state of being, an inner stability that does not get shaken under the turmoils of the outer world? This is what Shanta rasa means in Indian philosophy: it is the serenity that facilitates true joy, Ananda, to surface.

The Resistance to Stillness

We live in an age that glorifies busyness. Success has a correlational measurement to health, whether one works hard, is seen working faster, or is seen doing several things at once. Stillness is usually labelled as unproductive, labelled as a luxury for monks or hermits. The Indian mode of thought offers the opposite direction.

The Yoga Sutras of Patanjali define stillness as the calming of mental fluctuations (Chitta vritti Nirosha). Without this stillness, our happiness remains fragile—buffeted by external events, people's opinions, and uncontrollable circumstances.

The Neuroscience Behind Being Still

While Indian sages have extolled the virtues of stillness for centuries, modern research is just beginning to catch up. Scientific studies of mindfulness and meditation reveal that a quiet mind promotes well-being, nurtures emotional resilience, and can even lead to structural changes in the brain that enhance focus and inner peace.

Those who actively cultivate stillness through meditation experience a shrinking of the amygdala, the area of the brain associated with fear and stress, while their prefrontal cortex—responsible for high-level reasoning and calm decision-making—grows stronger. That means stillness is not just a spiritual concept; it is a biological necessity for enduring happiness.

Stillness and Action

Many thinks of stillness as inaction; the Bhagavad Gita introduces another perspective: active engagement with the world while maintaining inward stillness.

Sthit Prajna means "steady in wisdom" and is what Krishna describes to Arjuna. Such a being glides through chaos with unshaken serenity, neither holding joy tightly nor averting his face from sorrow. Thus, stillness is not a retreat from life; rather, it is getting engaged with life fully without being trapped in it.

Three Kinds of Stillness

To integrate stillness deep within, we need to learn them on three levels:

1. Physical Stillness

In a hyperactive world, everything is in constant motion, one job after another. Simple, basic practices such as sitting in silence for several minutes a day walking mindfully or even controlling unnecessary physical gestures can bring about a sense of deep presence.

2. Mental Stillness

Our minds churn through thousands of thoughts each day, many of which are simply a repetition of unnecessary ones. Breath awareness, deep concentration, or mantra meditations all stand to help diminish this mental static and brighten clarity.

3. Emotional Stillness

This happens to be the most challenging type of stillness. It entails instant reactions to people, events, disappointments, and so on. Emotional stillness means observing our reactions before acting upon them: responding, rather than reacting.

Cultivating Stillness in Daily Life

1. **Practice Short Pausing** - Before replying to a text message, decision-making, or impulsive reaction to an event, take a three-second pause. This little habit effectively inhibits impulsive reactions out of habit.

2. **Establish Rituals of Stillness** - Introduce a few minutes every day to just sit in silence, away from distracting stimuli. This conditions the mind to become comfortable with stillness.

3. **Develop the Ability to Detach** - Never let your peace be dependent on something outside you. If a certain situation disturbs your peace, always ask yourself: Is that within my

control? If not, let it go.

4. **Breathe Mindfully** - The ancient sages believed that breath is a mirror of the state of mind; it is observed that slow, deep breath leads to calmness.

Inner Silence to Reveal Ananda

The greatest reason why India's greatest sages sought stillness is not as an escape but as an entryway to the deepest truth of life. In the Mandukya Upanishad, the word 'turiya' refers to the fourth state of consciousness, which transcends waking, dreaming, and deep sleep. It is a state of silent awareness in which the mind is completely still yet fully alive. This silence is not emptiness; it is pure Ananda.

Silence to us is synonymous with void, an antonym to sound and noise; in reality, silence is fullness. Only in that stillness can one hear the wisdom that has been drowned out by the noise of endless thoughts. It is in stillness that one truly touches who they are in their essence.

Stillness Towards Self-Realization

With restless minds resembling a lake disturbed by wind unable to reflect the truth with clarity, the great Advaita philosopher Adi Shankaracharya once described. The same mind, when still, becomes like a mirror reflecting the unchanging reality of existence. This is why the sages insisted that stillness was necessary to realize Ananda was achieving some kind of bliss.

Genuine stillness occurs not in momentary breaks from activities, but rather deep knowing, when the mind no longer seeks fulfilment outside because it has found completeness within. The Brihadaranyaka Upanishad declares:

"Where there is no other, there is bliss. Where one sees nothing else, hears nothing else, understands nothing else, that is the Infinite."

Ananda, therefore, is not something we gain; it is something that becomes revealed when everything that is distracting falls away.

<u>Subtle Layers of Inner Stillness</u>

In touch with the physical or mental level, stillness gradually progresses toward its highest manifestation, which is the innermost quiet that remains undisturbed even amidst activities. This much being said, this can be split into three layers:

1. **The Stillness of the Body: Grounding Yourself in the Present**

The mind reflects in the body. When the mind is disturbed the body tenses; when it is restless, the mind should beasts. As such, yogic traditions emphasize postures (asanas) which cultivate a steady relaxed state within the body. Simple practices such as sitting in a posture of meditation with a straight spine or slowing down daily movements build the foundation for internal stillness.

Practice: Notice how much of your day is spent hurtling around: slow down all your actions of walking, eating, or speaking and translate everything to your movements, which must reflect the calm you pursue.

2. **The Stillness of the Mind: Dissolution of the Mental Noise**

Threads are innumerable in place, drawing from sometimes impossible tangled hoards of imaginary worry, craving, or distraction. What do you suppose would happen if we could step back far enough to simply notice this? The sages taught that the mind is a river hanging with the flow, but one watching it without attachment will water clear up. For it has been misunderstood that meditation means ceasing the cognitive process; rather, it is a realization that one is beyond one's thoughts.

Practice: For the next time you have a thought, rather than getting engrossed in it just label it thinking to yourself. Let it flow past just like the grey cloud sailing across the sky, withhold identification with each thought in mind, and label the idea as it forms to self: "thinking." This subtle practice detaches you from the mind's chatter and brings profound stillness.

3. The Stillness of the Self: Becoming the Silent Witness

Deeper than the mind and the body is the stillness that dwells in the essence of all things: the is. In this state, one is no longer at the mercy of the powerful forces of emotion and circumstance but rests as the awareness that sees all things come and go. This is what the Upanishads designate as the silent witness, the unchanging Self. When you reach that deep stillness, you realize that the peace you sought was never from outside; it was the essence of your being all along.

Practice: Sit in silence every day for yourself and ask, who knows my thoughts? Who knows my breath? Instead of answering, just observe. You move from being identified with the mind to being deeper aware underneath it.

<u>Final Step: From Stillness to Ananda</u>

Sitting in stillness is one of the most practiced conditions for candidate training, but it does not free them from their binding serenities. It is surrender that completes it, an inborn quality of being which renders both stillness and Ananda because this is no longer something that you do in your being itself. This is Shanta rasa; whereby pure joy is born in profound tranquility.

The Taittiriya Upanishad describes the journey of fulfilment in five layers (koshas), Ananda maya Kosha being the deepest: the sheath of bliss. This means that beneath our mental noise and worldly attachments, Ananda is always present, waiting to be uncovered.

True stillness is not about pulling away from life; it is living with such fullness that nothing can unsettle or disturb. It is the clarity with which to engage in the world and grace with which to carry through challenges at discovering that from every fleeting joy and thorny sorrow, there is an underlying bliss that is never disturbed.

And when you find that, you no longer search for happiness. You have become it.

The Unshaken Mind Has Power

Stillness is not about escaping life but living it more and more fully. From the most untroubled mind, one sees all these things just as they are no distortion, no fear, no ceaseless desire. And when we reach that state of mind distillation, there is no more desire for ephemeral joy. There's an experience of Ananda, the deep, unshaken joy that has always been within us.

SIX

THE ROLE OF PERCEPTION – SEEING THROUGH THE LENS OF REALITY

Everything you know about happiness, suffering, and fulfilment is only perception: What if the reality you live in is a projection of your mind?

People, in belief, see themselves as viewing reality as it is. However, ancient Indian philosophy holds a different stance, which is that one does not see reality; rather there is something filtered by perception, bias, and conditioning such as a huge set of mental filters that form one's experience. Unless one looks at these filters, one remains in an illusion (Maya).

Perception: Architected Experience

Back to the terms on how two people can see an event but feel something different. A farmer, for instance, may find happiness in a sudden rainstorm, while a city-dwelling soul rushing to work feels a rainstorm. Same event, different perception. The weight of simple truth itself is that events do not disturb, it is perceptions that do.

The Bhagavad Gita mentions in the lines of Krishna that perception plays a central role in the authenticity of human suffering and fulfilment. The wise do not become attached to such transitory feelings, for they understand that the worldly play itself is constantly changing. "As heat and cold, pleasure and pain come and go, so must you learn to endure them without attachment."

This detachment, though, is not indifference. It is a clear insight into reality, free from obscurations of personal bias and emotional turbulence.

The Three Levels of Perception

Like many things, Indian philosophy disintegrates perception into three levels of interpretation:

1. **Mithya Drishti (Illusory Perception)** - Viewing the world through fallaciousness and ignorance. Being caught within the conditioned thinking of society, without questioning, and blindly following everything.

2. **Vyavaharika Drishti (Transactional Perception)** - Practical, yet personal views and emotions hide under it.

3. **Paramar Thika Drishti (Absolute Perception)** - Seeing things as they are, beyond illusions, personal preferences, and fleeting emotions.

Most of us would operate on the first two levels, but the way to Ananda asks one to endeavor to transcend conditioned perception and see the world as it is.

Mind as a Filter: Conditioning Defines Reality

Each and everyone have a filter of their dawn till day, formed through culture, upbringing, experiences, and past impressions (Samskaras). This filter serves as the lens through which we view the whole interpretation of the world.

For example, someone who grew up in scarcity will always perceive lack when abundance is there. And someone who believes success equals happiness will sometimes feel empty even when everything on the outside is complete.

Indian philosophy incites us to realize those filters in mind. The Upanishads teach that the highest truth is covered, not by the world, but by the veil of ignorance that hides it. By lifting this veil, we experience Ananda- not as an intellectual concept but as a blended reality.

How to See Clearly: Breaking the Chains of Illusion

If perception is the root cause of the experiences we go through, then to change our lives, all we have to do is change our perception. Some of the ways to develop "Paramar Thika Drishti" include:

1. Observation Before Reaction

The first reaction assumes that the real truth of an event is to be determined by conditioning or some prior response. Stop. Observe. Question: Is this the only way to see this? A step backward shifts perspective and opens new dimensions.

2. Query the stories you live by

The stories we tell ourselves become our reality. Are you living by inherited beliefs you have outgrown? Challenge the assumptions that surround success, love, happiness, and suffering.

3. Develop a Mental Silence

The mind works continuously interpreting and labeling everything. Dhyana has been practiced for eons in ancient India to silence that internal noise and give direct experience, freed from meddling by inner chatter.

4. Transfer from 'Why is this happening to me?' to 'What is this teaching me?'

Contrary to resisting challenges, learning to frame them as avenues for growth would translate suffering into wisdom and obstacles into stepping stones.

5. See people beyond their labels

Most of us look at others through the lens of judgment. Learn to see the person beyond the role, opinion, or action; recognize what is common in shared humanity. This minimizes irrelevant conflict while enhancing intimate relations.

Ananda Through Clarity of Perception

Once the illusory clouds (Maya) of space are removed from reality, what remains is a deep, unshaken bliss. Ananda is not something which does exist; it is covered with layers of false perception.

The moment we stop distorting reality with our conditioned lenses, we realize that our fulfilment was never outside of us; it had always been in there, waiting to be seen. To see rightly is liberation, and real joy starts there.

The Vision that Brings About Ananda

The traveler in Yoga Vasistha, walking at dusk, suddenly freezes in fear. Before him lies a coiled serpent, its dark form barely visible in the fading light. His heart races, his breath quickens, and he takes a step back. But as the moon rises, its soft glow reveals the truth-it was never a serpent, only a rope.

This shapes our reality. The world, like ropes, simply exists, neutral and unchanging. However, the conditioned mind projects its fears, desires, and past experiences onto it, turning harmless ropes into terrifying serpents. Suffering arises from mistaking illusion for reality; peace comes with clear vision.

The highest obstacle to Ananda, according to Indian thought, is not external but the Avidya (ignorance) that distorts our perception. A passage in the Brihadaranyaka Upanishad encapsulates this belief: "As is one's knowledge, so is one's vision. As is one's vision, so is one's world." The implication is that our experience of life is not determined by events but by how we perceive them.

And so, the key to the opening of Ananda is not to change the world but to change our view of it.

The Liberation of Right Knowledge

The Mandukya Upanishad speaks of three states of consciousness:

1. Jāgrat (Waking Perception): The waking state sees the external world as absolute reality. We react to everything as it seems, taking for granted that what we see is the truth.

2. Svapna (Dream Perception): The dream state sees a malleable reality. However, we tend to remain enmeshed in illusion, clinging to impressions or stories spawned from our subconscious.

3. Turiya (Pure Awareness): The ultimate state, where perception is not clouded by any illusion whatsoever. Here, one sees things as they are, bereft of attachment, fear, or distortion.

Most of us operate between the first two states, mistaking our conditionally conceived thoughts and emotions for truth. But the path of Ananda will require that we move toward Turiya, where perception becomes clear and uncorrupted.

How the Impure Perception Causes Suffering

Imagine two people standing on top of a mountain at sunrise: One view refuse to take an awe-inspiring glance at the horizon and invokes a sense of something vast and infinite in him; the other, whose thoughts are occupied with emails and deadlines, hardly notices the exquisiteness of the colors in the sky. Same view, two entirely different experiences.

Why? Because perception is no passive thing; it is active in shaping reality. With a restless mind, we can't see beauty; with a serene mind, even the simplest of things becomes a matter of joy.

Suffering arises as false perceptual traps:

• Attachment to the Impermanent – That belief in something must last forever to bring happiness; we suffer when it changes. But the Bhagavad Gita reminds us: "That which is born must die, and that which dies will be born again." Nothing in the world is permanent except the Self.

• Seeing Pleasure as Fulfillment – Sensory pleasures are inherently transient, yet the mind clings to such experiences thinking that it perceives true bliss. The Taittiriya Upanishad teaches us that beyond bodily pleasure, there is peace of mind and beyond that is bliss (Ananda).

• Identification with Thoughts and Emotions – Thoughts are not facts. The mind tells stories all the time. Wisdom lies in discerning between observation and automatic acceptance of such thought patterns.

Seeing Beyond the Illusion: Practical Perception Shifts

1. Train the Mind to See Reality, Not Stories

In moments of suffering, ask yourself:

"Is this the truth, or is it my interpretation of the truth?"

Somebody spoke harshly to you, and your immediate impression is that they don't respect me. But, is that true?

Or, is that just a conditioned reaction? Perhaps they were in pain. Perhaps they were unaware of their tone. With this separation of truth from our thoughts, the pain starts to loosen its grip.

2. Awareness in Place of Reaction

Krishna describes the Sthit Prajna in the Bhagavad Gita, whose wisdom is settled. In such a person, impulsive reactions do not occur; there is a conscious response. This moment of delay before reaction brings forth different perceptions; this is a conscious choice versus a conditioned impulse.

3. From "This is happening to me" to "This is happening for me"

Instead of resisting challenges, shift to asking: What is this teaching me? Every experience, positive and negative, is molding you. That single change in perception ceases suffering and cultivates growth.

4. Watch Your Mind Without Identification

The Yoga Vasistha states: "The mind creates bondage; the mind creates liberation." You are not your thoughts. They arise and fade. You are the awareness that recognizes them.

Practice: Notice your thought processes during the day without attaching emotionally to them, like clouds crossing a sky. The more detached you can be, the clearer your perception will ultimately become.

When Perception Clears, Ananda Presents Itself

The great poet-saint Kabir has said:

"You run from room to room searching for the diamond necklace that is already around your neck."

That is Ananda: It is not somewhere outside of us but rather something that is obscured by our seeing. We clear the distortions of perception; Ananda reveals itself, joining the world in perfect harmony.

An individual with keen perceptions sees beyond loss and gain, beyond praise and criticism, and beyond fleeting emotions. They note that the world offers constant change, but that does not have to be true of their inner peace. They have found something deeper than happiness: An everlasting joy that is independent of what they see derives solely from how they see.

Thus, Ananda is not an expedition. It is not a rare occasion to be caught. It is simply reality observed in clarity.

SEVEN

NISHKAMA KARMA-THE SECRET TO LIVING EFFORTLESSLY

Deep within the Bhagavad Gita, there is a profound teaching, which overturns the very way by which we have understood action and success. Nishkama Karma literally means action without attachment to fruits. This teaching will invite us to involve ourselves in our duties with full dedication while being averse to attaching importance to the outcomes of our duties-'nishkama' or free from desire and suffering, fights for liberation from the cycle of desire and suffering.

The Essence of Nishkama Karma

Derived from Sanskrit, Nishkama means "without desire," and Karma translates to "action." They denote, "Actions performed without any anticipation of gain for oneself." This is karma-yoga, or "the way of action", wherein selfless action is regarded as a means for attaining liberation (moksha) in the spiritual dimension.

So, Krishna gives Arjuna the advice: "You have a right to action, but never to the fruits of action." This teaching renders the idea of engaging in activities without attachment to the outcome. Don't mind the result; it leads to mental tranquility and inner peace.

The Burden of Attachment

Success in modern life is what people constantly seek success that is recognized by society in terms of wealth. Happiness is hung on outside achievements. Things do not turn out the way we expect; disappointment, frustration, and even dire despair. Living such a life, one fact emerges: being attached to outcomes weighs heavily on you in times of peace.

As we fixate on the fruits that follow our actions, we become subjected to the dualities of success and failure, pleasure and pain. This alone depends upon our state of mind and how we see the situation because beyond that point, the attachment does not cloud our judgment, but leads to actions that are taken with more self-driven motives rather than genuine intent.

The Great Irony

All other factors aside, the most important problem with the pursuit of control is dealing with anxiety. It happens whenever we unearth all possible avenues of outcome dictation, and ironically, things just slip away in the opposite direction. This paradox, however, indicates that one's real concern, if he is looking for true mastery, does not lie in the control of any outside condition but in his internal responses.

To this, Nishkama Karma teaches us that we should learn to take the action itself and let go of all attachment to its outcome. To surrender our attachment to fruits is to align us with the natural current of life. In doing that, we allow ourselves some friction against life, which would otherwise have brought us some peace of mind.

Going Beyond Ego: beyond Selfishness

At its essence, attachment is quite simply ego, that is, the "I" and "mine." The ego always looks for validation and fulfilment, judging the worth of things based on their criteria outside of one's inner integrity. That reality alone restricts our potential and causes unintentional sabotage in our efforts toward real satisfaction.

Moving beyond the ego, embracing Nishkama Karma, from selfish desires transforms into selfless service. When action is performed as a duty and in devotion without gain in mind, then it is an expression of the higher self. Such action purifies the mind and leads one to spirituality.

Rendering Nishkama Karma to Life:

Incorporating Nishkama into daily living requires one to consciously shift one:

1. Do Everything with Devotion: Enter into your obligations, personal and professional, with an open heart and inner focus without obsessing over results. This single-minded engagement makes the quality of your actions even higher.

2. Cultivate Detachment: Remind yourself that you can act, but the results are rarely yours, and because of it you will learn acceptance and lessen anxiety.

3. Attitude of Offering Actions as Service: The work we are called to perform becomes more than something boring

when viewed as an offering, a contribution to something much greater than oneself.

4. Endure Unpredictability: Such is life-adaptability, and the willingness to bend and flow even when there is no real cut-and-dry answer about what to expect.

5. Reflect and Meditate Regular: These will allow the person to be self-aware and be detached through constant reflection and meditations, paving ways to observe thoughts and emotions with less entanglement.

The Release of the Life of An Effortless

Nishkama Karma frees us from shackles and the endless pursuit tied to validations outside ourselves. Liberation does not demand inactivity but a deeply engaged living mind at ease. Therein would lay more effective actions distanced from distortions of fear and greed.

It is, however, easy to adopt effortless living: by ordering our will to the natural scheme of things, performing flawlessly our duties and responsibilities, and loosening the strings that bind the need for control over results. This has given a lot of peace and gratification for the individual, closer to the state of real bliss.

Nishkama Karma is wisdom from Tapasya that has survived the test of all times and is timely for us here and now in a fast-moving world that holds results above all else. It tells us to reevaluate our definitions of work, success, and fulfilment. For in practicing action without attachment to results, we discover a way toward inner peace that ultimately culminates in joy, wherein true happiness is not found in the conditions of life realized at the edge but rather in having been integrated and detached from the performance of life duties.

To Ananda Through Action Without Self:

And when we think of happiness, we find ourselves at times too busy in this direction chasing after achievements, approval from others, and external rewards. Our Karma is tied up with what we call success and worth, and we measure ourselves in terms of the outcomes of our labors. However, as we have seen in the teachings of Nishkama Karma, true fulfilment does not arise from the fruits of our labor; rather, it emerges from the process itself, at which point action is performed without attachment to the result.

The Gita declares: "You have the right to carry out your duty but are not entitled to the fruits of your actions." Detachment from the burden of success or failure opens multiple doors to inner happiness and spiritual evolution. The next question is: Now how do we make this line of philosophy into an active principle that will lead us to the Ananda, a blissful state that exists independently of all external circumstances?

The Freedom of Letting Go of Results

To be a true Nishkama Karma practitioner, one must cultivate a recognition that attachment to results originates from one's grief. In this modern world, we are conditioned to identify success with measurable outcomes: money, fame, and achievement. But these external measures are fleeting; they are miscalculating judging discs of measure. When we pin our happiness onto exterior circumstances, we have lost both the real opportunity and the desire for one state.

When one pushes such a realization, he learns the essential elements of Nishkama Karma: freedom from the urge for outcome burdens the human mind with dissatisfaction. True freedom, however, is measured by the quality of one's action, not by the absence of action. Actions that flow out of duty and responsibility toward a larger cause, unrewarded by personal considerations, are true expressions and manifestations of the higher self—the realm of life flow.

The Dance between Effort and Surrender

Nishkama Karma teaches us this beautiful balancing act between effort and surrender. Many think that to achieve great things, one must exert relentless effort and control. However, true mastery is found in knowing when to act and when to surrender the results. The key lies in performing actions with dedication and commitment but without a grasping mentality. This balance allows us to go with life's rhythm, without forcing or resisting.

In the Gita, Krishna refers to Karma Yoga as the yoga of action that brings us into sync with the laws of nature that govern the universe. When we act knowing that the fruits do not reside in our hands, we engage with the demands of life with greater ease and grace. This is effortless living; a state in which the current of our efforts flows with the natural order.

Nurturing the Heart of Service

The very essence of Nishkama Karma is selflessness. When we act not for personal gain but for the benefit of others, our actions bring forth pure joy. Selfless action is love and compassion, giving of oneself without expectation of a return. With this orientation, every act becomes a gift, from the simplest task to a moment of kindness to the most significant contribution to our fellow human beings' well-being.

When we shift our mindset from "What will I gain?" to "How can I serve?", we align ourselves with the higher purpose of life. Service becomes the way of life— a constant reminder that we are all interconnected and that our happiness is dependent on the happiness of others. This view radically transforms our attitudes toward work, turning every job into an instrument of spiritual advancement, a ladder rung toward Ananda.

Transcending the Ego: The Path to Inner Peace

Egos go after attachments; Ego brings an awkward and false sense of separation; Ego goes for personal gain and gratification. Nishkama Karma sets us on a course to transcend this godhood. Stepping beyond the limitations of the ego and attaching purely to the activity of Nishkama Karma, one establishes a relationship with the infinite aspects of his true self.

This transcendence of ego does not mean the abandonment of self—it means recognizing that our true identity is not defined by what we achieve or possess. The more selflessly we act, the more barriers dissolved that the ego has created around our perception of Self. The enjoyment of bliss and profound peace will follow when this sense of boundary dissolves, for we shall become one with all that is.

Living Sync with the Universe: The Flow of Life

In nature, every action is a small thread woven into one great harmonious complete system. The river flows and takes nothing for itself. The tree gives fruits not for itself but for others. In Nishkama Karma, too, we come in alignment with the universal flow. We perform actions in life, knowing that we are channels of a stream much greater than ourselves.

Living in sync with the universe allows us an experience of Ananda flowing, which is consummately effortless. When we no longer resist what naturally ought to occur, when we act in clarity and peace, life movement comes without effort. Life passes by undisturbed, devoid of stress, frustration, and impatience, effortlessly and fulfilled. We are not burdened by stress, frustration, or impatience; instead, we move through life with a sense of ease and fulfilment, trusting that each moment is as it should be.

The Path of Selfless Action Leading to Ananda

As this philosophy shifts the emphasis from outer success to inner completion, Nishkama Karma defines the path to Ananda. Through actions done without attachment, we unchain ourselves from the mental strife caused by desire and expectations. As we do this, we begin to feel the joy that is always streaming beneath the pathway of life.

Ananda is not some distant achievement; it is already hidden inside us behind the covers of attachment and ego. When we unfasten the grip of wanting to control, when we give up the wish for certain results, we are restored to a state of peace, fulfilment, and joy. This is liberation, not liberation from action but liberation in action.

Knapsack for Nishkama Karma

Practical steps for incorporating the wisdom of Nishkama Karma into daily life:

1. Acting right now in the present moment: Every action you take, no matter how small or simple, is an opportunity for practicing Nishkama Karma. Be it working, eating, or even talking to someone, focus entirely on your present experience and let go of any thoughts that keep pulling you toward the future.

2. Letting Go of Results: In doing any task, remember that the result is not in your control. Out of this will be born pure attention to your effort, not the result.

3. Become Useful: Offer as much of your day to serving others without expecting anything in return. By doing this, you will transform all your existing mundane tasks into something profoundly spiritual.

4. Accept Doubt: Life offers little certainty. Search through your heart for the acceptance of the unknown, the stream of surrender, and trust that all is becoming however so.

5. Ask Yourself Why: Continuously consider the actions you take and what motivates them. Are those actions motivated by ego or selfless service?

Art of Effortless Living

Nishkama Karma opens before us the door to effortlessly live our lives. Doing duties with dedication, free of desire, one finds never-ending torment between success and failure. Thus, he becomes a worthy instrument of the Divine, gliding along the natural flow of life where Ananda spontaneously arises.

True fulfilment doesn't lie in the fruits of our actions; rather, it lies in the peace within ourselves, which we find in the process of living. Living without attachment, without expectation, and being in tune with service brings us joy which is the essence of our very being.

In this state of Nishkama Karma, happiness is something that is not an aim; it is a status or a way of life that transcends dualities of pleasure and pain, which is where Ananda thrives.

EIGHT

DETACHMENT WITHOUT INDIFFERENCE – A LIFE FULLY LIVED

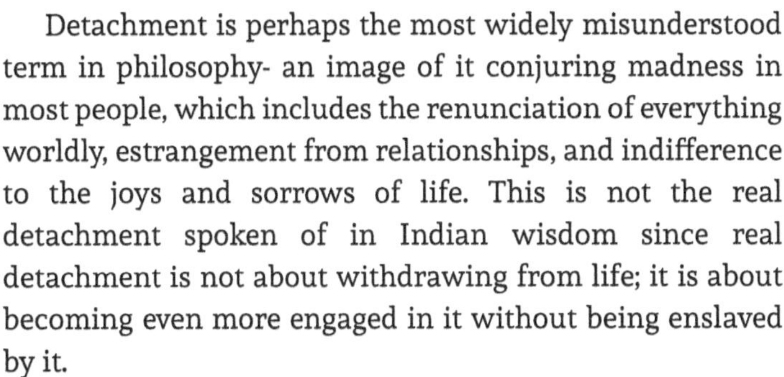

Detachment is perhaps the most widely misunderstood term in philosophy- an image of it conjuring madness in most people, which includes the renunciation of everything worldly, estrangement from relationships, and indifference to the joys and sorrows of life. This is not the real detachment spoken of in Indian wisdom since real detachment is not about withdrawing from life; it is about becoming even more engaged in it without being enslaved by it.

Why We Fear Detachment

We resist detachment because we equate it with loss; we fear if we detach, that we will no longer care, feel, or love. Such falsehoods maintain the ego, which thrives on attachments-whether to people, success, possessions, or identity.

Actually, it enables a much deeper and purer contact with life. It's to a life that strongly feels even while staying unaffected by a turbulent sea of changes. It's like being in the ocean but not doused in its waves.

The Balance Between Holding on and Letting Go

Most people either hold life too close to them or completely withdraw from it. But wisdom lies between indifference and attachment. According to the Bhagavad Gita, one should be completely engaged in action but inside free from attachment toward the result. This fact is simply the key to peace and effectiveness.

If you want to imagine it: hold sand in your palm. In a tight grip, it slips through your fingers. But if you hold it gently, it remains. This is life: to hold it gently.

Where Attachment Roots In: Why We Struggle in Letting Go

1. The Illusion of Control – We think that if we hold tight, we are in control of outcomes; yet, life is uncertain, and clinging creates suffering.

2. Fear of Emptiness – Without attachments, life will seem empty, we think, but real meaning comes from within and has nothing to do with outside dependencies.

3. The Ego's Identity Crisis – They give identity. Letting go threatens the ego's illusion of itself.

Living with a Detached Engagement

How do we practice detachment without falling into indifference? How do we care deeply, yet not get consumed? The answer is shifting the focus from ownership to participation clinging to flowing with life.

1. Love Without Possession

Attachment is not love. But love at its highest should not own a person nor rely on anyone to bring happiness. It is better to accept the person's totality with the awareness that they must be free to be who they are.

2. Work Without Anxiety

To more, most people work under failure or success obsession. You do best but realize the results don't lie entirely with you. That means shedding all stress and making the effort more efficient.

3. Experience Without Addiction

Enjoyment doesn't conflict with detachment. Good food, music, or relationships can be enjoyed without being enslaved to them. The key is to savor without craving more or having fear about losing.

The Ultimate Freedom

When you live in detachment, you move through life with ease relating deeply but not clinging, giving your best but not being broken down by setbacks, and loving to the fullest extent but not demanding. This is not indifference; this is true liberation.

The river flows effortlessly because it does not cling to the rocks. Life becomes effortless, too, when we enter into participation with presence, but keep ourselves free within.

The Deep Joy of Detached Engagement

One of the truest paradoxes in Indian wisdom is found in the fact that detachment is being fully engaged yet knowing an intensity of deeper, unshakable connection to life. Not indifference or withholding; rather, an invitation to participate entirely without being controlled by outside conditions. This variety of detachment is fully experiencing life with its joys, hardships, and uncertainties while remaining anchored in a deep, unshakable joy that comes from within.

The Road to Ananda through Detachment

Ananda, true bliss, comes from being freed from pipelines of attachment. But detachment is not abstinence from life and its pleasures: it is not renouncing relations, work, or experiences but also the ability to have all of those without letting them define a life. Detachment is key in how to live a fulfilled life, where joy is not in circumstances but is inherent in the way we engage the world.

The Freedom of Being Present Without Ownership

To live life embracing detached engagement is to wholly suck in life without actually hanging on to it. The ancient Indian texts, especially the Bhagavad Gita, speak of Karma Yoga: yoga in action where action is devoid of any being attached to its outcomes. Krishna tells Arjuna: "Perform your duty, but do not get attached to the results." This is key to a free and wholly liberated life. We are called not to abandon our duties or responsibilities, but to perform them with full presence, with full dedication, while letting go of the need for control over the results.

Then, as one frees himself of attachment over the outcome, he is no longer at the mercy of his desires, expectations, and disappointments. Instead, we are free to act from clarity because true joy comes not from external outcomes, but from the quality of our engagement.

Transformation of Loss into Freedom in Love

We no longer fear loss when we practice detachment. It does not mean that we have stopped loving or caring; on the contrary, it will deepen our loving and caring with more freedom, without needing to possess or control. True love is not ownership or expectation, but the presence of another and allowing him or her to be who he or she is without trying to shape into our own desires. This is the path to Ananda, about loving freely, giving freely, and enjoying the present without attachment to it.

Work Without Anxiety: A Dance with the Universe

Also here, detachment transforms experience in work. There are things, of course, that we hesitate to approach due to the dread of failure, insufficiency, or not coming up with the desired outcome. But relinquishing this fear places us at work in an effortless but almost strong manner. The disengagement is not from the world, but working with deep purpose and dedication minus the anxiety about the outcome.

Nishkama Karma: the teachings in Bhagavad Gita, remind us, that the fruits of labor are not in our hands. What we can hold is the effort to apply our intentions in work. When we give up any attachment to its consequences, we will be working much more sharply, creatively, and easily. This is the meaning of detachment: acting wholly present without the yoke of expectation on oneself.

Use Without Addiction: Savoring Every Pleasure in Life

Detachment can also imply that it allows for all of life's pleasures without their becoming addictions. A world of ever-accumulating consumption encourages and entitles actual detachment enjoyment of consuming without demanding more. Simple things such as eating a meal, listening to a beautiful tune, or enjoying the lovers' company are all consumed and relished, leaving no room to crave possession or repetition.

This is not deprivation from pleasure but rather experiencing pleasures that life has to offer without anything controlling us. The difference between enjoying something and addiction and grasping it can be articulated in terms of experience. An addicted individual would be one who chases pleasure filling the emptiness that is left within. A detached individual, on the other hand, experiences that pleasure just flows as part of existence; he does not cling to it or go around chasing it endlessly.

Method for Living with Ananda and for Inner Freedom of Detached Engagement

This is, in fact, the true object of detachment. To awaken to the deep unshakable joy found when we dismantle the ego's needs for control, approval, and possession. When we don't define ourselves in terms of what lies outside-us-achievements, relationships, or material possessions set ourselves free from fluctuations that result from the external world. We become rooted in the seed of joy that constantly exists within the self, independent of anything outside itself.

Surrendering to life with detached engagement frees us from the natural rhythm of life. We've learned not to fight change or control every situation; rather, we learned to engage fully with whatever comes our way, knowing that our essence remains untouched. Entrance into this freedom leads towards Ananda.

Living through detachment has been shown to people to experience real happiness and rather chase after joys because, in true freedom from that dependent attachment, the possessor of true joys is aware that all happiness lies deeply in one's self. That is, living each moment fully giving himself to true life: loving, working, and enjoying without identification. In fact, this really is the path of Ananda because, here, we experience profound peace and satisfaction, which is not subject to the changing conditions of life.

The Real Key to a Well-Lived Life

This means that living the life of Ananda through detachment is understanding that nothing in this world could give anything he is capable of having from within himself. The external world may come and go, but the delight derived from such a life of detached engagement remains constant. Excuse us, for we do not need to control, possess, or attach to anything. We do not need to live fully, without fear, without expectation, and without the need to hold on.

Detachment thus opens the very door to a life lived in its fullness. It is not avoidance or indifference to life but living life in the most profound engagement with the world free from the bonds of attachment. Ananda falls into that space where everything is there spontaneously, naturally, and eternally.

NINE

THE TRIAD OF SAT-CHIT-ANANDA – EMBODYING TRUTH, CONSCIOUSNESS, AND BLISS

In the Indian corpus of philosophy, the notion of Sat-Chit-Ananda is like a guiding light for the seeker, for it can lead him or her to the ultimate state of fulfilment and bliss. This trilogy - Sat (Truth), Chit (Consciousness), Ananda (Bliss)- offers a complete structure for understanding the nature of existence and its pathway toward such expansive happiness.

Sat: The Essence of Truth

Sat is the eternal truth underlying the universe; it is the reality derivatively absolute, wherein all things change.

Sat stands as the everlasting truth amidst the reality of transience in the material world; it is the truth that must be realized through discriminating between real and unreal: that which is permanent from that which is ephemeral.

Setback in true life is chasing after momentary pleasures or losing vague ones taking them to give real fulfillment. But even on rare occasions, they afford that durable happiness. Once one has held on Sat, attention has shifted from transience to eternity, thus defining selfhood from the unchanging truth.

Chit: The Light of Consciousness

Pure consciousness-"chit"-is that consciousness which makes us aware of the items in our experience. How is it the capacity to conceive, know, and think about the world and oneself? "Chit" may be cultivated by pure self-awareness and self-consciousness transcending egoistically.

Meditation and mindfulness practices can help tame the incessant talk of the mind and allow people to enter into that direct relationship with pure consciousness, which will allow people to observe thoughts and emotions without attachment and a sense of inner peace and clarity around them.

Ananda Being Bliss

Being in resonance with both Sat and Chit brings about the natural state of bliss called Ananda. It is not an event but rather deep joy and happiness that transcends even circumstance-the essentially proper experience of bliss realized through the knowledge of one's true nature and ultimate unity with reality.

Liberation of an individual self, says Taittiriya Upanishad, is the highest degree of Ananda, or bliss. This bliss is Brahman, the supreme being to which every human being is directed throughout life.

Integrating Sat-Chit-Ananda into Daily Life

To embody Sat-Chit-Ananda is a conscious effort to align thoughts, actions, and perceptions with truth, awareness, and bliss. Here are daily practice steps of integration of the triad into direct living.

1. Find Truth in Everything That You Do: Try to be honest and straight in all communications. Most of all, question assumptions and delve deeper into understanding to bring yourself closer to the essence of Sat.

2. Develop Awareness in Mindfulness: An active practice of nurturing your consciousness with enhancing practices such as meditation, journaling, or contemplative reading goes into nurturing Chit and creating the relationship with your inner self at a deeper level.

3. Embrace Happiness No Matter What: Happiness in reality is not brought about by something from outside. Happiness, true happiness, comes from the inner self and the eternal truth. Under this intensity of Ananda, circumstances do not matter.

From Bondage into Freedom

Indeed, it is a journey without. Ananda is the journey within and self-unfoldment. It means stripping oneself of the ignorance covering the true nature of oneself. As one aligns with Sat and intensifies Chit, the inevitable byproduct is the bliss of Ananda.

This is not giving up life in the world, but dealing with it from a place of deeper knowledge and awareness. This knowing that leads to compassion, purpose, and deep happiness transforms the lives of people.

Idealistic Framework of True Fulfillment

To create a life outside of such transitory pleasures and reach out to the eternal joy, that is at the heart of existence, is the very essence of India's lost philosophy of the art of fulfillment. By becoming truth, expanding consciousness, and embracing the inherent bliss of our being, we can transcend pleasures that are transitory. Thus, we can reach the fruition of the state of Ananda.

Awaken at the Ananda Triad

This triad Sat-Chit-Ananda does not refer to any theoretical conception; it is a practical guide to the fulfilment of a happy life. In fact, these three principles - Truth (Sat), Consciousness (Chit), and Bliss (Ananda) - are the foundations of existence as well as the path to final rest. When a person is living in accordance with these three, he will have an awakening to Ananda, or bliss beyond external circumstances, which reveals what true joy is.

Awakening Process into Truth (Sat)

Every day we face the onslaught of distractions that prevent us from accessing the truth. Illusions and ignorance ensnare us into chasing after momentary pleasure and validation from outside. But as it is, one has to pursue Sat, the constant truth, through saying no to the transient and seeking the eternal.

1. The Truth of Self:

To begin having that experience called Sat, one would need first to grasp the truth of who one is. Apparently, the Upanishads talked about Atman, which should not be equated with the body, mind, or emotions as the true self of a person. It is the essence of consciousness, eternal, unchanging. Such recognition would free an individual from the ego's endless pursuit of definition through social labels or roles.

2. The Truth of the World:

Thus, to be in Sat is to recognize that the world is impermanent. Everything in it is temporary-not just relationships and possessions but even our own bodies.

When we stop identifying ourselves with such impermanent things, we will begin to experience the eternal. This does not mean we have to renounce the world; it just means we do not get deluded into thinking that it is anything but a very real expression of the divine-hence powerfully shifting, but grounded in a singular truth.

3. Integrity in Action:

In practical terms, adhering to Sat is living truly and living integrous; for when we act in alignment with truth, then we do not need to manipulate or deceive to feel secure. The result, which is Ananda, is that we enjoy that much inner peace and truthfulness finely integrated within ourselves.

Chit-to expand consciousness to pure consciousness:

Chit is the next dimension in itself, the same calling the mind to witness the eternal truth so that the world beyond the narrow confines of the ego becomes apparent to us. Thus, we quiet the mind and go beyond the habitual patterns of thought that form our everyday lives.

1. Meditation as a device: it expands consciousness:

Meditation, the best practice for Chit, stops our minds, clears pathways beyond the ego, and connects with pure awareness, which is our true nature. We will be able to stand apart from our minds through actions in meditation and realize that we are not our thoughts, but those thoughts are there. We have a strong view of what we are conscious of for those that we witness. This window is through which we experience the world with clarity and presence.

2. Self-awareness Beyond the Ego:

The ego builds on these few visualizations, conditioning from the past, fears, and desires. Expanded consciousness would lead beyond the limited law of the ego. By periodically engaging in mindful practices like breathing exercises or self-inquiry, we unconsciously expand the awareness of who we are to include all of existence—the cosmos. This expansion leads to a very deep experience of interdependence with all beings and the universe itself.

3. The Light of Awareness in Everyday Life:

Chit can be part of what we do as Chit brings to mind. The idea isn't to retreat from this world but to bring every action under conscious control. If we eat, work, or engage with others meaningfully, then we can do it mindfully and in the present. This adds meaning even to the most mundane activities as expressions of consciousness such that even the simplest moments could give rise to great joy.

Living the Ananda of Being:

The ultimate end of coming into alignment with Sat and Chit is Ananda: the bliss that springs from living in consonance with the truth of one's being and with the awareness of one's embeddedness within all life. Ananda has nothing to do with momentary sensations or pleasures but with that deep, abiding joy that emerges in the absence of momentary jolts of mind and body.

1. Ananda as Natural State:

Ananda is, pure and simple, the essence of who we are. It is there within us already, waiting to be perceived, rather than something to be earned or acquired. The ultimate state-attitude, the highest experience of the self-Ananda is thus described in Taittiriya Upanishad: freedom from the need for validation through others or achievement transforms the blissful state into Ananda through alignment with Sat and Chit.

2. Joy of Being Present:

Ananda is the experience of living in the now. Life comes to be lived as it is simple, beautiful, and whole we are fully in the now with no attachments to the past or future. Work, relationships, or development done from presence gives rise to the immediate experience of an unending joy that is always available.

3. Giving Up Control to Surrender:

An important constituent of Ananda is the renunciation of wanting to manage the outcome of life. Letting go of one specific attachment to results allows one to be carried and floated with life. Surrender here is not a sort of passive resignation but very much active participation in this the best way we have, all we have given rise to life as it should unfold.

Incorporating the Triad into Daily Life:

Sat-Chit-Ananda teaches that the concepts taught within it may not be limited to some abstract subjects to reflect on alone but should rather be integrated into every aspect of our lives. Here are some practical ways in which this triad can be put into action in our everyday lives:

1. Seek the Truth in Everything:

Ask if all this is for truth, as daily life passes: in work, relationships, or personal interests, remain aligned with your Puritan principles. Ask in everything that you do for a more profound understanding of being real, for being real aligns actions with the eternal and grounds one into Sat.

2. Develop Mindful Awareness:

Begin your day by practising mindfulness every day: meditation, deep breathing, and reflection. Throughout the day, at moments when you pause to reflect on what is happening in your thoughts and electromagnetic field, remind yourself that you are actually not your thoughts as awareness constructs this expansion of consciousness. In this way, you live in Chit.

3. Enjoy Being: Recognize that actual bliss does not depend on many outward achievements or conditions. It

is found in simply bringing oneself and everything around into a present moment of life. Relate fully to every moment, and discover the natural joy that comes with presence.

Life living in the Triad of Sat-Chit-Ananda

It gives no clearer plan than Sat-Chit-Ananda for a life well lived. Truth becomes an expression of life, consciousness evolves, and we embrace the bliss that is part of our very nature, transcending the passing pleasures of the material world to encounter the eternal joy at the essence of existence.

As you integrate these principles into daily living, remember that Ananda is not some distant end; it is already a state of being, present within you. You align yourself with Sat (truth), Chit (consciousness), and Ananda (bliss), and wake up into a life of deep fulfilment, peace, and joy. This is the essence of the philosophy of fulfilment lost in the Indian art-the road leading to the ultimate Ananda.

In the Indian corpus of philosophy, the notion of Sat-Chit-Ananda is like a guiding light for the seeker, for it can lead him or her to the ultimate state of fulfilment and bliss. This trilogy - Sat (Truth), Chit (Consciousness), Ananda (Bliss)-offers a complete structure for understanding the nature of existence and its pathway toward such expansive happiness.

Sat: The Essence of Truth

Sat is the eternal truth underlying the universe; it is the reality derivatively absolute, wherein all things change. Sat stands as the everlasting truth amidst the reality of transience in the material world; it is the truth that must be realized through discriminating between real and unreal: that which is permanent from that which is ephemeral.

Setback in true life is chasing after momentary pleasures or losing vague ones taking them to give real fulfillment. But even on rare occasions, they afford that durable happiness. Once one has held on Sat, attention has shifted from transience to eternity, thus defining selfhood from the unchanging truth.

Chit: The Light of Consciousness

Pure consciousness-"chit"-is that consciousness which makes us aware of the items in our experience. How is it the capacity to conceive, know, and think about the world and oneself? "Chit" may be cultivated by pure self-awareness and self-consciousness transcending egoistically.

Meditation and mindfulness practices can help tame the incessant talk of the mind and allow people to enter into that direct relationship with pure consciousness, which will allow people to observe thoughts and emotions without attachment and a sense of inner peace and clarity around them.

Ananda Being Bliss

Being in resonance with both Sat and Chit brings about the natural state of bliss called Ananda. It is not an event but rather deep joy and happiness that transcends even circumstance-the essentially proper experience of bliss realized through the knowledge of one's true nature and ultimate unity with reality.

Liberation of an individual self, says Taittiriya Upanishad, is the highest degree of Ananda, or bliss. This bliss is Brahman, the supreme being to which every human being is directed throughout life.

Integrating Sat-Chit-Ananda into Daily Life

To embody Sat-Chit-Ananda is a conscious effort to align thoughts, actions, and perceptions with truth, awareness, and bliss. Here are daily practice steps of integration of the triad into direct living.

1. Find Truth in Everything That You Do: Try to be honest and straight in all communications. Most of all, question assumptions and delve deeper into understanding to bring yourself closer to the essence of Sat.

2. Develop Awareness in Mindfulness: An active practice of nurturing your consciousness with enhancing practices such as meditation, journaling, or contemplative reading goes into nurturing Chit and creating the relationship with your inner self at a deeper level.

3. Embrace Happiness No Matter What: Happiness in reality is not brought about by something from outside. Happiness, true happiness, comes from the inner self and the eternal truth. Under this intensity of Ananda, circumstances do not matter.

From Bondage into Freedom

Indeed, it is a journey without. Ananda is the journey within and self-unfoldment. It means stripping oneself of the ignorance covering the true nature of oneself. As one aligns with Sat and intensifies Chit, the inevitable byproduct is the bliss of Ananda.

This is not giving up life in the world, but dealing with it from a place of deeper knowledge and awareness. This knowing that leads to compassion, purpose, and deep happiness transforms the lives of people.

Idealistic Framework of True Fulfillment

To create a life outside of such transitory pleasures and reach out to the eternal joy, that is at the heart of existence, is the very essence of India's lost philosophy of the art of fulfillment. By becoming truth, expanding consciousness, and embracing the inherent bliss of our being, we can transcend pleasures that are transitory. Thus, we can reach the fruition of the state of Ananda.

Awaken at the Ananda Triad

This triad Sat-Chit-Ananda does not refer to any theoretical conception; it is a practical guide into the fulfilment of a happy life. In fact, these three principles - Truth (Sat), Consciousness (Chit), and Bliss (Ananda) - are the foundations of existence as well as the path to final rest. When a person is living in accordance with these three, he will have an awakening to Ananda, or bliss beyond external circumstances, which reveals what true joy is.

Awakening Process into Truth (Sat)

Every day we face the onslaught of distractions that prevent us from accessing the truth. Illusions and ignorance ensnare us into chasing after momentary pleasure and validation from outside. But as it is, one has to pursue Sat, the constant truth, through saying no to the transient and seeking the eternal.

1. The Truth of Self:

To begin having that experience called Sat, one would need first to grasp the truth of who one is. Apparently, the Upanishads talked about Atman, which should not be equated with the body, mind, or emotions as the true self of a person. It is the essence of consciousness, eternal, unchanging. Such recognition would free an individual from the ego's endless pursuit of definition through social labels or roles.

2. The Truth of the World:

Thus, to be in Sat is to recognize that the world is impermanent. Everything in it is temporary-not just relationships and possessions but even our own bodies. When we stop identifying ourselves with such impermanent things, we will begin to experience the eternal. This does not mean we have to renounce the world; it just means we do not get deluded into thinking that it is anything but a very real expression of the divine-hence powerfully shifting, but grounded in a singular truth.

3. Integrity in Action:

In practical terms, adhering to Sat is living truly and living integrous; for when we act in alignment with truth, then we do not need to manipulate or deceive to feel secure. The result, which is Ananda, is that we enjoy that much inner peace and truthfulness finely integrated within ourselves.

Chit-to expand consciousness to pure consciousness:

Chit is the next dimension in itself, the same calling the mind to witness the eternal truth so that the world beyond the narrow confines of the ego becomes apparent to us. Thus, we quiet the mind and go beyond the habitual patterns of thought that form our everyday lives.

1. Meditation as a device: it expands consciousness:

Meditation, the best practice for Chit, stops our minds, clears pathways beyond the ego, and connects with pure awareness, which is our true nature. We will be able to stand apart from our minds through actions in meditation and realize that we are not our thoughts, but those thoughts are there. We have a strong view of what we are conscious of for those that we witness. This window through which we experience the world with clarity and presence.

2. Self-awareness Beyond the Ego:

The ego builds on these few visualizations, conditioning from the past, fears, and desires. Expanded consciousness would lead beyond the limited law of the ego. By periodically engaging in mindful practices like breathing exercises or self-inquiry, we unconsciously expand the awareness of who we are to include all of existence—the cosmos. This expansion leads to a very deep experience of interdependence with all beings and the universe itself.

3. The Light of Awareness in Everyday Life:

Chit can be part of what we do as Chit brings to mind. The idea isn't to retreat from this world but to bring every action under conscious control. If we eat, work, or engage with others meaningfully, then we can do it mindfully and in the present. This adds meaning even to the most mundane activities as expressions of consciousness such that even the simplest moments could give rise to great joy.

Living the Ananda of Being:

The ultimate end of coming into alignment with Sat and Chit is Ananda: the bliss that springs from living in consonance with the truth of one's being and with the awareness of one's embeddedness within all life. Ananda has nothing to do with momentary sensations or pleasures but with that deep, abiding joy that emerges in the absence of momentary jolts of mind and body.

1. Ananda as Natural State:

Ananda is, pure and simple, the essence of who we are. It is there within us already, waiting to be perceived, rather than something to be earned or acquired. The ultimate state-attitude, the highest experience of the self-Ananda is thus described in Taittiriya Upanishad: freedom from the need for validation through others or achievement transforms the blissful state into Ananda through alignment with Sat and Chit.

2. Joy of Being Present:

Ananda is the experience of living in the now. Life comes to be lived as it is simple, beautiful, and whole we are fully in the now with no attachments to the past or future. Work, relationships, or development done from presence gives rise to the immediate experience of an unending joy that is always available.

3. Giving Up Control to Surrender:

An important constituent of Ananda is the renunciation of wanting to manage the outcome of life. Letting go of one specific attachment to results allows one to be carried and floated with life. Surrender here is not a sort of passive resignation but very much active participation in this the best way we have, all we have given rise to life as it should unfold.

Incorporating the Triad into Daily Life:

Sat-Chit-Ananda teaches that the concepts taught within it may not be limited to some abstract subjects to reflect on alone but should rather be integrated into every aspect of our lives. Here are some practical ways in which this triad can be put into action in our everyday lives:

1. Seek the Truth in Everything:

Ask if all this is for truth, as daily life passes: in work, relationships, or personal interests, remain aligned with your Puritan principles. Ask in everything that you do for a more profound understanding of being real, for being real aligns actions with the eternal and grounds one into Sat.

2. Develop Mindful Awareness:

Begin your day by practising mindfulness every day: meditation, deep breathing, and reflection. Throughout the day, at moments when you pause to reflect on what is happening in your thoughts and electromagnetic field, remind yourself that you are actually not your thoughts as awareness constructs this expansion of consciousness. In this way, you live in Chit.

3. Enjoy Being: Recognize that actual bliss does not depend on many outward achievements or conditions. It is found in simply bringing oneself and everything around into a present moment of life. Relate fully to every moment, and discover the natural joy that comes with presence.

Life living in the Triad of Sat-Chit-Ananda

It gives no clearer plan than Sat-Chit-Ananda for a life well lived. Truth becomes an expression of life, consciousness evolves, and we embrace the bliss that is part of our very nature, transcending the passing pleasures of the material world to encounter the eternal joy at the essence of existence.

As you integrate these principles into daily living, remember that Ananda is not some distant end; it is already a state of being, present within you. You align yourself with Sat (truth), Chit (consciousness), and Ananda (bliss), and wake up into a life of deep fulfilment, peace, and joy. This is the essence of the philosophy of fulfilment lost in the Indian art-the road leading to the ultimate Ananda.

The Practice of Fulfilment

TEN

THE SPIRITUAL SCIENCE OF EVERYDAY LIFE

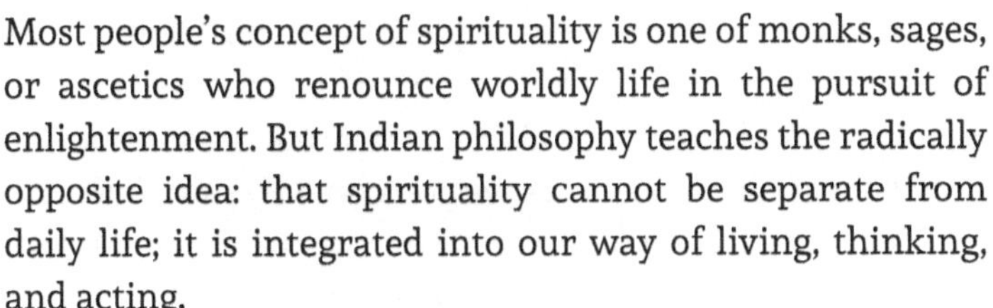

Most people's concept of spirituality is one of monks, sages, or ascetics who renounce worldly life in the pursuit of enlightenment. But Indian philosophy teaches the radically opposite idea: that spirituality cannot be separate from daily life; it is integrated into our way of living, thinking, and acting.

Attainment of Ananda—an ultimate state of fulfillment—need not demand his very escape from the world, for it can actually be cultivated by rendering each ordinary experience into a very deeply spiritual act. The secret is to bring awareness, intention, and alignment into the very little moments of our lives.

The Myth of Spirituality as an Escape

Many believe that spirituality is about rejecting the material world, detaching from society, and spending life in solitude. Such an idea arises from a stupidly limited view of spiritual practice. To be truly spiritual is not to escape life, but to enter it completely, with clarity, awareness, and grace.

While Krishna does not encourage Arjuna to give up the battlefield in the Gita, he teaches him to engage in his duty with wisdom and detachment. In a similar way, we are not meant to abandon our responsibilities, but to be aware of them on a deeper level. Ananda cannot be found in escaping from life—rather, it is found in the very midst of it.

Three Pillars of Everyday Spirituality

Indian philosophy provides three guiding principles that facilitate the integration of spirituality into daily life. These principles are far from being theoretical; they represent practical insights that can transform our experience of mundane existence.

1. **Karma Yoga**—Finding the Divine in Action

With complete awareness and selflessness, even the simplest actions can become a pathway to fulfillment. This is Karma Yoga—the path of action. If we fill the act with presence and intention and free our mind from the selfish attachment for an outcome, we can turn any mundane...

Most mundane actions can be transformed into a sacred experience with this inner change of perception: offering every task as a gift. Picture doing your work, not as a burden, but as a contribution to the world, a form of service from and expression of your inner self. The secret to Ananda is not what we do, but how we do it.

2. **Bhakti Yoga**: The Love of Man as a Path to Transcending the Void

Much of the modern teachings emphasize mindfulness and discipline but sometimes lack the emphasis on love and devotion that is so potent. Bhakti Yoga teaches that it is via the love of existence, of people, of life itself that we can develop consciousness of higher states.

Bhakti means far breaking through ritualism. It means cultivating reverence and gratitude everywhere. When we are grateful for the beauty of the sunrise, appreciate a simple meal, or act kindly toward another human being, we are demonstrating Bhakti.

3. Jnana Yoga: The Wisdom of the Mundane

Every experience is a lesson. Every problem is an opportunity to increase our understanding. That is the way of Jnana Yoga: to further cultivate awareness through wisdom and self-inquiry. Instead of thinking of life as a meaningless procession of events, Indian philosophy teaches us to see order, meaning, and interconnection.

As we begin to question our assumptions, notice our thoughts, and ponder our experiences, we become wise from the inside out. To live Jnana Yoga means to ask again and again: What is this moment wanting to teach me? What illusion am I holding onto? Where is my awareness right now? It is such simple questions that will lead us to greater clarity and self-realization.

Turning the Mundane into the Sacred

Ananda does not include only exceptional moments; it is concealed in all the simplicities of life. The way we drink a cup of tea, listen to the wind, or engage in day-to-day conversation could be their mechanical act in the opposite of being highly spiritual.

• Eat with awareness—taste the food, be grateful for the nourishment.

• When walking, walk with awareness. Feel the weight of each step; notice the air on the skin.

• When you talk, talk from the heart. Speak words of integrity and kindness.

· When suffering comes, watch without clinging; accept, adapt, and learn.

It grows with awareness of the divine in the concrete and the everyday events.

The Inner Stillness-the Science

Slowing the mind brings clarity and well-being, according to modern neuroscience, and ancient sages have taught that for centuries. Scientific studies about being deep-headed and meditative start activating the parasympathetic nervous system, lessening stress while heightening focus.

That way, while practicing inner stillness, we begin to respond, rather than react, from insight instead of impulse. And with this, we maintain a composed presence along the journey of life.

In such a moment in time, to be dragged by the external circumstances, one accumulates Ananda, being an anchor, whose state of unshaken life s waves pays no heed to the temporary whirlwind of the ups and downs of life.

Ananda in Today's World

With speed, combined with productivity, efficiency, and achievement, the modern world finds spirituality to be a radical alternative to presence, awareness, and Ananda. The loss of this great art, that of fulfilling life, is the loss of doing lesser; instead, it is to be present, aware, and connected.

For Ananda, one is not to transform their outside life, but only to change how the mis interact with it.

God lives inside the heart that beats each minute and everywhere else where every possibility is manifested.

Living the Life of a Spiritual Scientist

Spirituality is not an addendum to life; it is life itself, an experience lived with awareness. Every moment, encounter, and chore can serve to awaken one to a deeper truth.

To be spiritual does not mean to renounce the world, but to embrace it fully—with clarity, wisdom, and love. It means seeing the extraordinary within the ordinary, the infinite within the finite.

Realizing this awareness of daily living, one will understand that Ananda was never lost; it was always around, waiting to be recognized.

Everyday Action with Secretly Hidden Spiritual Power

Ananda, the most profound and lasting satisfaction that could be reached within the depths of the heart, could be concealed in the ordinary-the everyday rituals and simple acts of living-rather than those extraordinary moments, in meditation or seclusion. There are lessons from the lost wisdom of India's spiritual practices that every moment and every action offer a point of awakening to the divine within. This section of chapter will lead us to tap on that colossal potential: converting a life lived in daily grind into one where each day is part of a spiritual practice given over to transcendent transformation.

Reconnecting with the Divine in Daily Tasks

Although nowadays, when we zoom through life, or rather, when we rush through the fast lane of life, spirituality exists in quiet reflections or a formal celebration and not through action. The Ananda is really in the activity between this and that-the task we have chosen to attend to. It actually-gives a thousand channels to the flow of highly powered spiritual energy in every activity that we perform, as described in the Bhagavad Gita. By bringing awareness to everything we do, we will turn the banal mundane into the sacred.

1. The Sacredness of Routine: Presence in the Ordinary

Think of waking every day with reverential Ness towards the activities lined before you. These three actions-such as cooking breakfasts, replying to emails, going for a walk-could be transformed into practice not burdens, but opportunities to practice presence. When you approach each thing fully, you connect with the present rather than get lost in future expectations or deep past regrets: This is where Ananda is found-realization that joy and fulfilment are not connected to occasions but in our being now.

2. Transform Your Thinking: From Task to Offering

Every action, no matter how small, may become an offering. This is the heart of Karma Yoga-the yoga of action performed selflessly. You do not need to renounce your work or hobbies; it is about infusing them with intention and mindfulness. The way you approach your work, your family, and your community can become a vehicle for spiritual growth when performed with a sense of service. Ask yourself as you engage with each task: "How can I offer this moment as an expression of my higher self?" Ananda does not lie in what you do but how you do it.

Through Love and Reverence to Life (Bhakti Yoga)

3. The Way of Loving: Bhakti Yoga Beyond Rituals

When understood this way, all acts, events, and experiences are ritualized, and thus, everything and everyone is imbued with deep meaning and purpose. That is why love becomes the central point in Bhakti Yoga; love makes a power transformation of a particular personalized experience into a spiritual one. Not the love which possesses and treats people less than human, but the love which gives freely and sees the divine in everything; the love through which we will unlock even deeper levels of Ananda.

One can really start practicing Bhakti Yoga in the daily life by simply seeing God in the ordinary moments-an interaction which one can consider as a reflection of love-listening with understanding, giving a random act of kindness, or simply sharing a smile with someone else. When you encounter others with that depth of reverence bestowed upon them, at least a niche for Ananda is there, naturally emerging into your living space. This type of love converts normal life into the Divine.

4. Gratitude: Pathway to Delight

Gratitude is one of the most potent doors through which Ananda is unlocked. The moment one lives with a keen sense of gratitude in both the large and small blessings of life, thereby allowing for much more of a divine reservoir of love and joy to flow into oneself. Start admitting already existing gifts, whether it's a roof, food, or relationships. Bhakti is thus seeing God in everything, living with open hearts, and seeing divinity in simple things instead of rituals alone.

5. Mindful Awareness: The Wise Practice of Self-inquiry

Jnana Yoga-the path of wisdom-is about acquiring knowledge that liberates through self-inquiry and discerning the nature of reality. This does not involve pure philosophical study, but rather the cultivation of constant awareness about thoughts, feelings, and actions. Every moment brings a situation that teaches wisdom; every moment also can awaken the deeper truths of life, as one brings mindful awareness within experience.

Ask yourself: What is this moment teaching me? What is my mind holding onto that prevents me from experiencing peace? Every challenge, every setback, and every relationship are an opportunity to question the assumptions and beliefs that shape your reality. The more you engage with life in this way, the clearer your understanding becomes, and with it, the deeper your connection to Ananda.

6. Nurturing the Witness's Mind

Jnana Yoga teaches us to stand aside from thoughts and emotions and watch them without attachment. And in that process of learning, we come to recognize that we are not our thoughts; we become the witness to our experiences. That is the practice of this detachment, not a dissociation from life but an observation of it with clarity and equanimity. It is here in such space-of-detached-awareness that Ananda dawns upon a person because in this space, he is not attached to the transience of thoughts, emotions, or external events.

Integrating Spirituality into Everyday Life

This is true spirituality: it is not an aspect of life; rather, it is woven into every action, every relationship, and every moment. Ananda would not be gained in withdrawal or solitude; it is inherent in how we live, how we love, and how we engage with the world.

Karma (action as worship), Bhakti (devotion through love and reverence), and Jnana (wisdom through self-awareness) would create life in terms of a sense of really rich spirituality and depth. The lost philosophy of the art of fulfillment in India elaborates it as spiritual science, wherein one is, not is doing.

Awakening to Ananda in Every Moment

The Ananda is not something to be realized in some distant future; it is here now, within you, waiting recognition. Ancient Indian wisdom instructs that by vialing the ordinary and pervading the present moment with mindfulness, love, and wisdom, we fall in line with the divine flow of life.

In daily life, once you have worked the spiritual science in Ananda, you stop seeing it as a momentary emotion but rather as something at peace and joy with fulfilment for the greater part; a life truly lived, not to escape anything, but rather to embrace life with clarity, awareness, and deep connection to the truth of who we are.

ELEVEN

HOW TO BUILD INNER RESILIENCE WITHOUT HARDENING YOURSELF

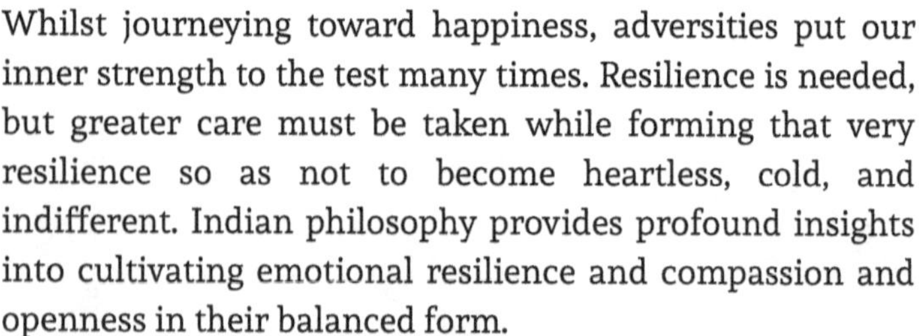

Whilst journeying toward happiness, adversities put our inner strength to the test many times. Resilience is needed, but greater care must be taken while forming that very resilience so as not to become heartless, cold, and indifferent. Indian philosophy provides profound insights into cultivating emotional resilience and compassion and openness in their balanced form.

Essence of Resilience in Indian Thought

In Indian philosophy, resilience isn't just about bearing the adversities but about regarding them as the doors of opportunity for growth within. Many Indian philosophers use an important word to express their opinions on the subject: Shaniya (enduringness; tolerance; endurance; resignation). But the ultimate practical application, sadhana—an instrument of limitless possibilities within a virtually boundless human consciousness—repeatedly throws one's own self into the power of the mental speculations which assure the temporary and the transient. An amazing blend of resilience combined with contemplation; description may change but the application level of the same never does; part consists of this element of generation of mental blocks, or Samadhi. The resilience and continuity of these blocks—definitely predicted on an exceptional study in comparative philosophy—is called Titiksha. This simple psychological summary cannot be equated to what one naturally achieves in the process of contemplation of the Absolute.

Non-Dual Phenomenal Universe of Titikṣā

The concept of Titikṣā, put forth in the Vedānic philosophy, means enduring life's dualities without complaints and despondency. It is about accepting the transient nature of experiences and maintaining inner tranquillity in the face of turbulence due to external forces. The attitude illustrated in Titikṣā encourages resilience among folks by urging that they face life with patience and calm acceptance toward obstacles.

Balance between Detachment and Compassion

The common misconception says that emotional detachment is a prerequisite for resilience. However, in Indian philosophy, the more balanced view is to be compassionately engaged with the world yet remain nonattached. This balance is cultivated by self-regulation and the acknowledgment of the impermanence of emotions.

Practical Steps to Foster Resilience

1. **Self-Reflection**: An Individual becomes well aware of his emotional responses, under self-reflection, and is then able to strategize ways to manage them effectively.

2. **Mindfulness Practices**: Mindfulness fosters self-awareness and emotional regulation, hence giving resilience.

3. **Embrace Impermanence**: Seeing that everything is inherently impermanent helps in reducing attachment and developing a balanced perspective.

4. **Community Support**: Connecting with people provides emotional support and reinforces resilience.

By incorporating these practices, an individual can develop a stronger yet compassionate inner resilience that leads to the fulfilment of Bliss Reich Ananda.

The Path to Morality through Resilience and Engaging with Compassionate Strength

So, the path to Ananda comes with buoyancy, gleam, and vivacity but is probably desolated if resilience stands silently and attempts to reduce humanity. The true spirit of resiliency does not reside in hardening itself against challenges but rather in cultivating a heart sacrificially patient with grace and compassion. In highlighting the steps leading toward emotional resilience, Indian philosophy is not just teaching the art of resisting pain but showing the art in transcending all forms of pain through living out one's life in compassion.

Resilience Beyond Hardness: The Heart of Strength

Resilience is often misconstrued as being stoic, as "smiling externally and bearing internally." Obedience to the law of altruism calls us to make an effort against difficulty with tender feelings rather than without it. The Bhagavad Gita does not teach Arjuna to detach himself from or suppress emotion in the battle; it teaches him to do so rather with an awareness of himself according to the knowledge that life is subject to change and that Ananda ultimately emerges when his change is considered.

This is where Titikṣā, the practice of endurance, plays a transformative role. Rather than hardening ourselves in the face of pain or challenge, we are taught to practice endurance by embracing hardship as part of the divine flow of life. The mind that is resilient is not one that shuts down or avoids pain, but one that faces hardship with patience and wisdom.

Power of Compassionate Resilience

In the development of emotional resilience utmost care must be taken not to confuse detachment with being indifferent. The balance lies in fully engaging the world with compassion but not being overtaken by the turbulence of external circumstances. It is a strongly advocated perspective in Indian philosophy that life and its difficulties must be encountered fully with a kind heart, and on this compassionate engagement rests the greatest power.

Let us take the example of a tree in a storm. It bends and sways with the wind, not breaking at all. Its resilience lies not in fighting the storm but in changing by adapting. Similarly, emotional resilience is not about becoming indifferent or distant but about reaching the strength to live through various engagements in life without the definitions of respect or the emotions defining them.

Building Resilience without Hardening: The Balance of Engagement and Detachment

Building resilience of the heart is not necessarily about detachment, as is often mistakenly thought in Indian philosophy. It implies recognition and understanding that the very nature of life circumstances is impermanent, and the further understanding that our emotional states keep changing constantly. Just as one is aware that the season changes, one also has to accept and be prepared to accept at a stroke the fluency of one's emotional modulation. From the viewpoint of resilience—that is, from the vantage point of an individual who willingly and wholeheartedly but without any crack in his/her engagement with the world experiences all manifest junctures of life—a living philosophy has time and time again proved itself.

Lord Krishna, in *Bhagavad Gita* instructs Arjuna to participate actively in work but without being emotionally attached to its fruits. This perspective makes a flavor of universality—that we can work, love, and feel intensely, all the while unaware that nothing will outlast us. Thus, it keeps us resilient since we know that realities change but do not harden when those changes come along with the fluctuating nature of emotions and situations, into the understanding of it.

Practical Pathways to Cultivating Resilience with Compassion

1. Self-Invite Efficient Search: Investigating Source of Emotional Responses

First, other sources of emotion need to be revealed through self-discovery and reflection. This is true also in forming compassionate resilience since through self-introspection, one discovers one's beliefs, fears, and conditioning through which responses are shaped to challenges. This practice in the Indian spiritual texts is Atma-vichara, or the self-inquiry aspect. The notion of observing without judgment those emotional triggers is the starting point to the larger understanding in which this strength, wherewith a response is chosen, can be found in the understanding of how certain triggers exist for certain responses.

For instance, "What does this trigger in me? Why do I feel hurt?" When thrown by criticism, we ask for ourselves instead of being defensive, thinking about triggers, and hence separating emotional from identity causation, allowing important thinking instead of impulsive responses.

2. Develop Mindfulness as an Emotional Regulation Tool

Mindfulness, or Smrti, is perhaps the most powerful quality of human beings, or transforming minds, in relation to the above-mentioned emotional resilience. Mindfulness teaches awareness of thoughts, feelings, and sensations in the body without being clinging to them. Little gems in our daily life for action in a moment of stress or emotional turmoil would be sailing through stopping, observing, and responding with clarity and intention, without being carried off with the flood of emotions by that instant.

And, as an example, here might be one practice: noticing anxiety and frustration and then stop immediately taking a second to breathe deeply and just notice the feeling. Not judging it, nor trying to push it away; just acknowledge its being. Observing without attachment renders us able to experience our emotions without being crushed under their weight.

3. Cultivate Impermanence.

According to Indian philosophy, everything in a life is temporary--happiness and misery, success and failure. This understanding lets one sit balanced, knowing that no feeling or mode remains eternal. Hence, this makes one free from negative feelings and enables one to face problems as just transient phases of growth.

In fact, remind self, what "this too shall pass" means whenever overburdening. Indeed, it brings us to the knowledge of impermanence. Resisting or controlling the natural flow in life is releasing in itself. It promotes change and actually increases resilience in our lives. It gives us greater opportunities for peace and contentment.

4. Strengthening Kinship Ties

Recognizing oneself and forging personal practices to meet adversity are vital ingredients in building resilience. Being surrounded by a supportive network of like-minded people, whose values you share and who provide you with emotional assistance when you are faced with adversity in life, is crucial in overcoming life's challenges. Lord Rama had this in the Ramayana: Resilience for him came from himself and other people he galvanizes together to help him fight his challenge.

Pick people who raise and energize you. Choose, as well, relationships that come from mutual respect, empathy, and understanding. Such human connections provide him emotional nurturing, therefore keeping him strong but also open to compassion.

The Inner Strength of Compassionate Resilience

Resiliency or strength combined with compassion represents the ability to live resiliently in a world that needs, and of course, full of hardship. Resilience is not closing up emotionally or withdrawing from all things worldly, but it does entail a capacity to embrace all life's ideas in an open heart and a steady mind. This strong manifestation arises from Titikṣā-the endurance of life's dualities with patience and from the realization that everything is impermanent.

As you follow this path, remember that Ananda comes not from escaping hardship but from facing it with resilience, wisdom, and compassion. The foundation for true fulfillment is then laid through this process of crafting this resilience, one dependent neither on external circumstances nor on other people's perceptions but results from strength and peace within.

Fulfillment in Resilience

Cultivating resilience, then, isn't about hardening the heart or detaching oneself from what life offers. It is about fostering the strength to stand firm with an open heart, balanced perspective, and no wavering commitment to growth through adversity. This kind of resilience leads not only to emotional fortitude but to Ananda, the deep peace that arises when we can experience life to the fullest without being overwhelmed.

Incorporating all the lessons in Titikṣā, mindful engagement with life, and compassion transforms our failings and difficulties into opportunities for growth and joy. And in that process, one learns that true appreciation is not about avoiding difficulty; rather, it is in practicing with regard to all situations-including allergy of difficulty, in regard to it with grace, wisdom, and resilience. The way to Ananda-an inner peace and joy that is the greatest state is through all those paths.

TWELVE

THE SMALL JOYS THAT GO UNNOTICED

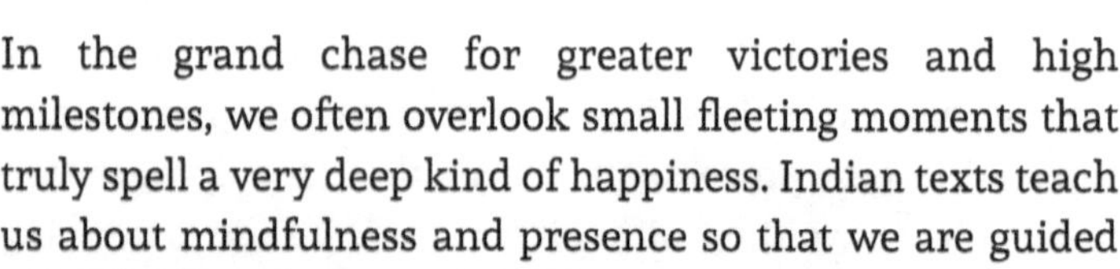

In the grand chase for greater victories and high milestones, we often overlook small fleeting moments that truly spell a very deep kind of happiness. Indian texts teach us about mindfulness and presence so that we are guided toward identifying and celebrating such small joys as pathways to Ananda—true happiness.

The Overlooked Essence of Daily Life

Society today teaches us to connect happiness with successes of big magnitude—promotions, flashy cars, or social accolades. The whirlwind of excitement that comes with such events may seem pleasurable, but all too often, they leave us wanting more. On the contrary, the small and subtle joys of everyday existence can bring us one's own lasting joy, if only we could pay more attention to those.

Mindfulness: The Gateway to Present-Moment Awareness

Mindfulness, a practice with roots in Indian traditions, engages ourselves completely with the present moment. With sustained practice of mindfulness, the distinctive features of our daily living are brought to attention, giving us scope for delight in almost everything that may appear to be trivial.

Another Way to Practice Mindfulness:

1. **Morning Rituals**: Let your day awake with a few minutes of silence and contemplation or with a meditative exercise. This sets an aware and grateful tone for the day ahead.

2. **Sensory Engagement**: Focus on the sensory details around you—the smell of your morning tea, the warmth of the sun on your skin, the sound of rustling leaves.

3. **Deep Listening**: While conversing with others, listen from the heart without prematurely crafting your response. This adds to the intimacy of connection while enriching the experience of human interaction.

The Philosophy of Contentment: Santosha

Santosha (contentment) is firmly established as one of the central observances in the Yoga Sutras. This helps us to find satisfaction with what we have rather than seeking it in everything external. Santosha teaches us how to enjoy some small joys given by life, day by day.

Implementing Santosha in Everyday Life:

• Maintaining a Gratitude Journal: Keep a record of joyous moments and the things you feel grateful for each day. This shifts attention from what is lacking to what is abundant.

• Simplifying Desire: Identify your needs and wants. The less confusion you have with your desires, the lesser your chances of being upset, thereby making it easier for you to be content.

Interconnectedness of All Beings

Indian philosophy speaks often about the interconnectedness of all life. With the awareness of this unity, one could find joy in oneself through well-being of others and the world around.

Ways to Embrace Interconnectedness:

• Practice Kindness: Engage in small acts of kindness, like helping a neighbor or donating to a local cause. These acts will not only help others but also give you a sense of fulfillment.

• Connection with Nature: Spend time in nature, observing the intricate relationships within ecosystems. This fosters a sense of belonging and appreciation for the interconnected web of existence.

Practicing Detachment: Vairagya

The practice of detachment, or Vairagya, deals with the release of all rigid expectations and excessive attachment to specific outcomes. This enables us to have a little more openness to small and unexpected joys that life may have in store for us.

Vairagya in Daily Life

• Letting Go of Perfection: Take a deep breath and smile; not everything will go according to plan. Make peace with imperfection and find beauty in the unexpected.

• Be Flexible: Be open; life will be richer for it! Strive to allow a situation to unfold without shackling it with stringent expectations from the start.

Walking the Subtle Road to Ananda

Ananda, or true fulfillment, is found not merely in the glorious accomplishments but much more in small, hushed moments of everyday life. It is cultivation of mindfulness, a practice of contentment, realization of interconnectivity, and the embrace of detachment that will open us to the resplendent glory of the commonplace. This way, we uphold the wisdom of ancient Indian philosophy: the path to everlasting happiness is interwoven through the day-to-day pursuits of our lives.

Finding Ananda in Small Quiet Moments

In the hurry of modern-day life, it is easy to forget that Ananda, or true fulfillment, does not lie in the loud, attention-grabbing milestones we tend to chase, but in the small, quite unnoticed moments that fill our daily life. Indian philosophy teaches us to look below the surface, to seek that joy which may be hidden deep in the smallest of experiences. The key to finding lasting happiness is awakening to the small, unnoticed joys that life offers-Diamond.

We can now unlock the doors to Ananda by means of mindfulness, contentment, and by embracing the fullness of every moment. From this point onward, the section guides you to cultivate a deep awareness of the small moments, how they serve as pathways to the fulfillment you seek, and how every day can become a deep experience of spirituality.

Sanctifying the Ordinary

Indian philosophy sees sacredness in everything; it is in the context of meditation and in rare life-altering moments that we may tend to see the spiritual. The real journey is to behold the divine in the most ordinary things. As soon as we begin to transcend our habitual ways of perceiving and begin to see beauty and interconnection all around us, we step into Ananda at every moment.

This recognition lies in the Dharma concept, in which we behold the divine. It is thus the beholding, not the scrying for something outside, rather the acknowledgment of divinity in ourselves and in everything around us. When we engage fully with whatever we are doing—working, cleaning the house, or having a conversation—all those actions start to become sacred actions.

The Power of Seeing Anew

Practice the art of darshan in your everyday life. Have the food that you are about to eat seem like a gift—it may become really awesome to think that way when you sit. When you relate to others, each interaction becomes a sacred exchange for the holy viewing. Through that lens, you will view life not as a string of incidents and obligations but as an open avenue for connection, presence, and joy.

The Inner Joy of Simplicity: Letting Go of the World to Give External Validation

Most of the time, the modern human tells him that happiness resides miles away from him and in the outside world's achievements-recognition, success, and wealth or status. Indian wisdom, on the other hand, states that the human being who actually attains fulfillment in simplicity, upon releasing himself from attachment to external validation. Embracing Santosha (contentment) and Vairagya (detachment), we learn to delight in quiet acceptance and presence, not in outside worldly achievements.

Contentment, actually, comes when one turns the external meter with which he or she usually measures happiness into the internal. Rather, this is being satisfied with what one has. Learn to appreciate the smaller simple gifts that life does provide. We simplify what our desires are, and finally, we are free to really enjoy the little moments, the true source of happiness that lasts.

Inner Simplicity

To give contentment to your life, you may first know the difference between needs and wants. Most of the time, it turns out that it must be, that happiness is what we really have at the moment when we stop chasing after things that will supposedly make us happy. Think of all the little things every single day-your health, your home, your people-and take time to be thankful for them. When practiced, gratefulness draws Ananda into life, reminding that happiness is generally more proximal than in things we do not often attend to.

Practice of Presence: Peace in the Now

Ananda is, hence, very much with the present moment. Unfortunately, in the bustle of modern life, we might get too much stuck in the past or project into the future-sometimes just ruminating regrets and sometimes anticipating desires. But the full experience of being in the present can only happen in the now. The practice of mindfulness, a hallmark of Indian spirituality, actually teaches being in the moment, savoring and being aware of every bit of it however trivial it is.

By learning to immerse ourselves fully in the present moment, we throw the doors of our life wide open to the treasures that might otherwise go unnoticed-particularly the taste of food, the air moving in and out of our body, or fleeting moments with others. In the happiest situations, these experiences can become sources of flourishing joy and fulfillment.

Practical Mindfulness

To be present, try engaging in just one exercise at a time, all out. Walking, eating, or talking with another person--whatever it is, immerse yourself fully in that experience. Feel your sensations, continue to notice all the little details around you, and forget about everything else. This practice has increased anchoring in the present, where small and usually hidden joys of life arise.

The Subtle Joy of Service: Finding Meaning in Giving

The truest joy comes from selfless service, one of the strongest, most solid tenets of Indian philosophical school. Those sacred Kindness and generosity with no strings attached bring about inner sync with the yet deeper flow of life. The joy of giving is lasting and transforms its transaction from mere fleeting to something deeper and real.

Just about all acts of kindness and service, big or small, join one with this greater whole of humanity. The service touches the lives of others and turns them into even such joy for us. This very interconnectedness nourishes our sense of fulfillment and reminds us that Ananda emanates from the world rather than from the pursuit of one's goals.

Small Serves in Daily Life

Look around your day to find opportunities to offer kindness; help a neighbor, lend an ear to a friend, or spare some time working for a cause. Kindness and service: little or big, each leaves a seed of joy inside your heart. This collection of small, insignificant things goes to build a happy life.

Letting Go of Attachments: Life Just Is

Vairagya shows one how to give up unwanted expectations and attachments to results. This doesn't mean becoming apathetic toward life; it means it's the art of letting a person move life along its own natural course without that one controlling everything. We are then liberated from trying to have everything follow our plan as we go with little unexpected gifts that come along life's way.

Accepting Imperfection

Don't go against or resist that which is out of control; instead, accept the imperfections. Let beauty and charm reign supreme in the unpredictability that is life. By letting go of the need for perfection and control, one creates a great space into which is allowed to flow the natural joy of acceptance that life is as it is.

Conclusion-Ananda Awakening in the Everyday

Anand is not unreachable or unattainable. It is a state when we notice and appreciate the small moments that fill up our daily lives. Through appreciation of presence, or embracing that all-important contentment, from selfless service, and also that giant release of attachment to outcomes, we open ourselves to the vast, abiding joy that is always findable in the present moment.

Reality: true art of fulfillment is recognizing that sacred small joys-an inner peace not ruffled by the outside noise, a quiet connection with the world, these little things. At the same time, mindfulness, gratitude, and divinity align the self with timeless wisdom revealing the way to Ananda. And there, it is discovered fulfillment is not something to be sought after; it grows in every moment we often live an unexamined life.

THIRTEEN

Letting Go of Control While Staying Fully Present

One of the greatest paradoxes in the search for Ananda is this: finding true fulfillment necessitates the relinquishment of control. The human mind craves certainty; it seeks to predict, plan, and manipulate outcomes to create the illusion of safety. But to live is to be unpredictable. No matter how much we strategize on our given aspects, there will always be elements under the radar of human exploration.

The Illusion of Control

Control is associated with stability in our collective consciousness. We draw meticulous plans, set firm goals, and try to mold our lives into what we fancy. Are things often done as we planned? The more we try to control our world, the more we suffer when it refuses to fit our expectations.

This illusion of control is akin to the veil of Maya in Indian philosophy; the illusion makes us think we can somehow seize and mold the external world into our liking. But Maya never is. Maya is temporal and ever-changing. To look for permanence in an impermanent world is to give birth to frustration and disappointment.

Surrender as a Strength, not a Weakness

Letting go of control does not imply surrendering to passivity or resignation. Surrendering is not about giving in. It is learning how to yield to the natural rhythm of life, trusting that the process may be smarter than we are. Surrender signifies that the divine intelligence is operating in and through us, all around us, and beyond us.

The Bhagavad Gita describes how Krishna instructs Arjuna to surrender all his worries and act with no consideration to result: "Abandon all attachments to the fruits of action, and find peace in surrendering to the flow of the universe." This is not an instruction not to act, but to act fully, consciously, and with presence but not be enslaved by the outcome.

Staying Present while Releasing Control

Letting go does not mean disconnecting from life; rather, it means engaging with life with 100% involvement while resisting nothingness. Here is how we can nurture this balance:

1. Control to Flow

Instead of forcing situations to conform to expectations, let them unfold. This embodies the cardinal concept of Wu Wei in the Taoist tradition, the effortless act of going with the flow once we stop swimming against the current of life.

· Be flexible when involved with planning. Hold goals lightly, allowing for change.

· Whenever complaints arise, take a pause before reacting. Ask, what is this moment teaching me?

· Let go of the illusion that things can only be "right" if they happen in a certain way. Very often, life's greatest blessings are disguised as unplanned detours.

2. **Accept Uncertainty**

Anxiety occupies our minds when we cannot sustain uncertainty; yet uncertainty is the very nature of existence. Rather than fearing it, we can embrace it.

· Every morning tell yourself: Today will be unpredictable, and that is all right.

· Practice adaptability. Cognitive adaptability allows resilience.

· Understand that uncertainty allows new possibilities to emerge-things we could never have imagined in the case life took a straight road.

3. **Engage With the Moment Completely**

Whatever happened has gone. What is yet to come has not yet come. The only place where life actually takes place is the present moment.

· Practice conscious presence during every day, routine activities-eating, walking, listening, or working.

· Deep breathing, focusing on the present moment, should guide an anxious mind back home again.

· Tell yourself: This moment is enough. Nothing is missing in this present moment when you are fully here.

The Joy of Letting Go

Imagine the liberation if we stop holding on, stop resisting, stop being afraid of change. Letting go, contrary to common perception, brings gain rather than loss.

· Gain the freedom to let joy become its own end, rather than accepting limitations imposed by life as an etheric dagger of hope.

• Freedom from attachments that hurt.

• Freedom to embrace life as it is versus how we think it ought to be.

The moment we stop clinging to our control is when we liberate ourselves and truly allow the universe's wisdom to guide us. We trust. We breathe. We merge with the flow of life. In this effortless surrender lies Ananda.

Incorporating Surrender into Everyday Life

Letting go is a slow practice; it is not an isolated act but a constant practice of awareness. Here are some suggestions on how to actively support surrender in daily life:

1. Observe Your Resistance

Become aware of those moments when you resist reality. Do you get angry when things don't turn out as you had expected them? Are you forever trying to make others conform to your needs? Realizing when you're in resistance is the first step in letting it go.

• Journaling helps reveal where control and attachment patterns exist.

• With meditation, the mind can witness observations without judgment and avoid engaging in negative thought streams.

• Waiting to respond creates breathing space for acceptance.

2. Small Acts of Letting Go

Start out with little, relatively easy actions.

• Let someone else choose the restaurant or movie for the night.

• Allow the conversation to flow without interference.

• When plans are altered unexpectedly, rather than lashing out, try stating: Let us see where this takes us.

These gradual changes train the mind to loosen its grip and trust life to unfold.

3. **Surrendering Is an Active Process**

The widely held misconception is that surrender equals passivity; simply put, that "just waiting" is the simplest definition of surrender. In reality, surrender means acting with focus without a spec of attachment to control. It is all about taking inspired action while also leaving space for life to sculpt results.

• Be purposeful in your movement, yet allow whatever outcome is best to happen.

• When setting goals, consider who will benefit from this. Just take care to detach from specific time frames.

• Trust that what is meant for you will come, and what is not will leave.

4. **Find Stillness Amidst Change**

In turbulent moments, harboring an inner stillness. The mind jumps in a defensive state to react; however, the deep wisdom rose from silence.

• Spend time with nature, observing how trees bend in the wind, yet stay rooted.

• Take slow, conscious breaths when stressed.

• Remind yourself: The world moves; I can stay steady within it.

5. **Recognize the Gift of Surrender**

Life surprises you in ways you could have never made happen when you stop resisting. The relationships that nourish you, the opportunities that present themselves effortlessly, and the moments of sheer joy-the gifts that come through surrender.

Look at uncertainty not as something to dread but an invitation to stretch yourself.

• Greatest breakthroughs happen when we stop forcing the solution.

- Greatest love experiences happen when we stop wanting to control another.
- Greatest peace is found when we stop fighting with life itself.

Final Note: To Live in the Flow of Ananda

Ananda is all about trust—trust in life, trust in the unknown, trust in the very intelligence of existence. Letting go is not a loss; it is a homecoming to a deeper, more natural way of being.

In this way, you no longer do struggle against life, but instead you now dance with it. With the letting go of control comes the discovery of freedom. And in that freedom will be your true fulfillment.

FOURTEEN

Living Ananda in the Modern World

FOURTEEN

THE DHARMA OF WORK – PURPOSE WITHOUT PRESSURE

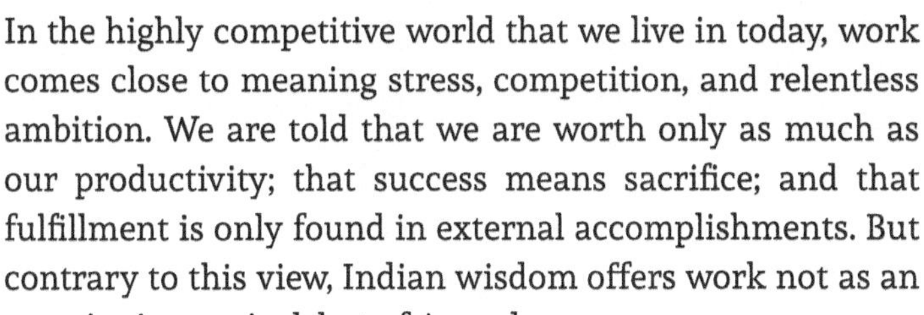

In the highly competitive world that we live in today, work comes close to meaning stress, competition, and relentless ambition. We are told that we are worth only as much as our productivity; that success means sacrifice; and that fulfillment is only found in external accomplishments. But contrary to this view, Indian wisdom offers work not as an exercise in survival, but of Ananda.

The old idea of Dharma thus serves as a basis for thinking anew about work. At its simplest, Dharma is right action-the instinctive duty one owes to oneself in accordance with one's true nature. When work proceeds in harmony with Dharma, it averts stress and enters the sphere of self-expression, service, and inner peace.

<u>The Conception that Work is a Struggle</u>

From a young age, society indoctrinates us into thinking of work as a means to an end. Promotions and wealth-building schemes have magically filled the horizon at the end of which lies recognition and satisfaction. Even if this orientation may have led to some success, it has ultimately breathed exhaustion and disappointment down our neck.

In contrast, Indian philosophy can place worth into work when one acts with an attitude conducive for such work to become fulfilling. Instead of working solely toward results, work is there to be enjoyed.

Krishna told Arjuna in the Bhagavad Gita: "You have a right to your work, but never to the fruits of your work." However, this is not implying to give up all kinds of goal setting and ambitions but to inform our striving with detachment. Full dedication with no obsessive attachment to outcome means joy and inner peace; stress and anxiety meet when we get attached.

Finding Your Swadharma: The Work Aligned with Your Nature

Dharma is not a rigid set of rules but one very personal thing. Swadharma stands for one's unique path—work that follows one's abilities, temperament, and higher purpose.

Some are born leaders; some teach; some heal, some create, and the list goes on. Only the alignment of work with Swadharma feels energizing rather than engendering a sense of burden or exhaustion.

To discover more about your Swadharma, pose the following three questions to yourself:

• Which activities satisfy me the most?

• What types of skills or talents do I find myself naturally gravitating to?

• How may my work focus not only on personal return but also on greater benefit?

Balancing Ambitions with Inner Calmness

Purposeful work guided by Dharma walks a thin line between ambition and surrender. When achieved through the ego or insecurity, blindly following ambition leads to complete burnout; once aligned with Dharma, it allows one's highest self to express itself effortlessly.

Indian philosophy does not advise surrendering ambition but refining it. Rather than seeking competence for external validation, instead seek the excellence in oneself. This change in perspective will free work from being perceived as a struggle and turn it into a meditation.

Work as the Path for Spiritual Growth

In the Bhagavad Gita, Krishna introduced Karma Yoga, or the path of selfless action. Work is no longer an option for survival or success; it is purified through work; it instills discipline and inner evolution.

When we actually let go of ourselves and give ourselves over completely to our work, sincere and dedicated, it becomes a part of the spiritual life. Mundane work, when performed in awareness, fosters inner development.

And so, a teacher in the transmission of knowledge; a farmer in the production of crops; an artist in the giving of beauty: All experience Ananda through their work, but only if they are working with presence and devotion.

How to Combat Stress and Resistance in Work

Many people feel imprisoned in jobs that do not resonate with their Dharma. From such jobs, however, we can build meaning out of that which is apparently unworthy of working towards. Changing the mindset from 'I have to do this' to 'I choose to do this' changes everything.

Some pointers for overcoming stress and resistance:

· Shift the focus from result to effort-based, in so doing: Have fun with the work rather than concern yourself with results.

• Add mindfulness to your work: Bring all your awareness to each task, and be present and intentional.

• Task consideration as service: Establish how your work impacts others and focus on making meaning for your work beyond personal gain.

• Establish a flow: Build a balance among work, rest, and contemplation to evade downhill fatigue.

This Ability to Work Well and Without Pressure

Work offers no fulfillment; the way in which we confront work will be the true source of fulfillment. The ancient wisdom of India informs us that work is neither punishment nor a race. It is an opportunity for nurturing one's inner potential.

Dharma cum freedom from devastating preoccupation with results plus the cultivation of joy in the process equals Ananda-the joy of working where the joy is within the work.

That is suffering-free art. Such is the Dharma of work: purpose without pressure, effort without exhaustion, and act of peace.

The Role of Service and Contribution in Work

Work, by itself, is for individual fulfillment. But more so, work has a greater function toward the collective well-being of society. What Dharma tells us is that true success cannot just be measured by individual achievement; it must also consider society and the world we live in at large.

1. Work that is a Form of Seva (Selfless Service)

Seva, or selfless service, one of the highest forms of work as per Indian tradition. It is work done without expectation of reward and done for others. Even in a job, work can maintain the spirit of Seva.

• A doctor treating patients with compassion

- A businessperson operating with ethics and integrity
- An artist creating for inspiration rather than just profit

When work is perceived as a contribution to others rather than just providing for oneself, it becomes a pathway for deeper fulfillment.

2. **Ego-less Work**

In large part, work stress arises from ego, from our need for recognition, comparison, or validation. Dharma asks us to relish the act of creation for the joy of seeing our work evolve, not for any accolades on a personal level.

- Get obsessed with mastery and cease to compete.
- Forget about comparing; your path is unique.
- View work as a gift rather than an obligation.

3. **Sustainability and Balance in Work-Life Integration**

A core principle of the Indian philosophy state that: only integration is meaningful and that work is not seen as an obligation detached from other obligations of personal growth, relationships, interactions, fulfillment, and inner well-being.

- Embrace periods of quiet contemplation!
- Pay attention to the body's natural rhythms: alternating between work and rest.
- Working for life, not for the moment!

<u>Final Insight: Work as a Lifetime Meditation</u>

With wisdom, work becomes a life into the meditation; without it, work becomes merely labor. One may talk much about the kind of work we do-not the work itself, but the spirit in which it is done.

To work living dharma is to be joyful working without stress. It is to find meaning, work, and pleasure in life, free of expectations.

This, however, is not mere philosophy. It is a lifestyle, and those who choose it will draw nearer to Ananda.

FIFTEEN

RELATIONSHIPS, LOVE, AND THE ART OF GIVING WITHOUT EXPECTATION

There is often confusion about what love really is. The societal hype has conditioned a belief that love is about possession, control, and expectation. In reality, love is freedom, trust, and selfless giving. In age-old Indian philosophy, real love is not about seeking fulfillment from others, but about sharing the fullness within us.

The Illusion of Possessive Love

In modern relationship love usually involves attachment. We tend to think that people will complete us, fulfill our needs, provide emotional support, and perform according to our desires. The reality is that attachment is not love; it is dependency within which arises suffering.

Everything in the Bhagavad Gita says that a true love should be driven in dispatchment. This detachment doesn't make both distance from one another but allows them to grow without the fear of loss. Too much grip closes love. The more space allows space for love.

Ananda Through Love: A Paradigm Shift

True love is an expansion of Ananda, that deep bliss that comes from within. It does not depend on another person to bring happiness. It not only exists but brings meaning into one's love life. When we cultivate happy feelings of self-sufficiency from ourselves rather than seeking happiness externally, we first find ourselves with the capacity to give unselfishly, and second, we undergo unconditional love.

• Instead of "What can I receive from this person," ask "What can I give?"

• Do not grip but know that love will flow through naturally.

• Not Control, but Free Space to Grow Out to Each Other in Relationship Commitment.

Ultimate Form of Love: Giving Without Expectation

Indian philosophy centers on Seva, selfless service, as the greatest love. Seva isn't just helping another person, but a way of life where we give freely, without holding the expectation of getting some reward in return. A few examples:

• A parent nurtures a child, expectedly without taking any appreciation.

• A teacher imparts knowledge without ownership to the student.

• A friend offers support without accounting for the trade-off.

That love would set people free from the ache of unfulfilled expectations. It teaches that giving is a joy in itself. The more we let go of constraints created by the necessity of reciprocity, the more love flows as if on its own.

Love and Dharma: Balancing Relationships

Dharma also translates into love, beyond emotional expressions. The relationship that is in accordance with Dharma is one that uplifts two people to each other, one who inspires the other to grow, and respects their difference in journey.

• Respect personal journeys: Each path has its own Swadharma; its unique purpose: Healthy relationships sustain this instead of conforming.

• Fearless love: Fear-based love will control, become jealous, and be insecure. Dharma-based love trusts the natural flow of connection.

• Commitment with a space of freedom: True commitment is not binding each other, but waking up to consciously choose each other every day without fear or obligation tied to it.

Overcoming Ego in Love

The ego constantly makes inquires Am I getting sufficient? Am I getting treated nicely? Am I getting enough love? All these questions with endless self-consciousness weaken love. To reach Ananda, love must be ego-free: from "I" to "we", self-centered desire to selfless giving.

Ways to dissolve ego in relationships:

• Deep listening-no preparing for what one is going to say next, just listen.

• Acts of Kindness-unnoticed, without the requisite of action, just because it brings joy.

• Being wrong sometimes matters-let go of the need to be right to understand rather than to win.

From Attachment to Liberation in Love

For most people, love tends to be defined as attachment; however, attachment is also the cause of fear—fear of loss, betrayal, or not being good enough. Love liberation comes to us when we realize that love is not for possessing but rather enjoying to the fullest in the present moment.

Freeing, giving, and aligned with Dharma is the highest fulfillment. Not dependent on any outside conditions, it is a manifestation of Ananda or bliss that was never outside but always within.

Cultivating Profound Relationships and Extending Love Beyond Oneself

The highest form of love must be transcendent in the relationship to all living beings. When love is viewed as an experience with the divine, then it starts becoming boundless. It is no longer restricted to one relationship but expands into every single interaction.

1. Expanding Love Beyond Romantic and Familial Ties

• Compassion as a Way of Life: Love is not something we give to close friends or partners. It's something we exist in. When we bring love into all our interactions-from a stranger on the street to a colleague at work-it becomes larger, even more expansive to experience Ananda.

• To See the Divine in Others: According to Vedantic philosophy, everyone is an extension of the same universal consciousness. Only then love becomes unconditional and all-encompassing.

• Forgiveness is Freedom: By keeping grudges, we bind ourselves to pain. Liberation from the past is not condoning wrongs that have taken place but liberating us from the emotional baggage.

2. The Practice of Maitri (Universal Friendliness)

Maitri, or loving-kindness, is a Buddhist and Hindu practice. It is the conscious cultivation of goodwill towards all beings, including those who may have wronged us. How to practice Maitri in daily life:

• Gift of silent blessings to that one meet, wishing them peace and happiness.

• Kindness towards difficult people. It takes effort to see what they are struggling with rather than reacting to them.

• Meditate on universal love by picturing oneself as a vessel infused with warmth and compassion.

3. Love as a Path to Self-Realization

Love, in Indian philosophy, is not just an emotion but a path toward attaining self-realization. The Bhakti tradition says pure love destroys the illusion of distinction between the self and the whole universe. In such case, love, when freed of expectation, becomes a form of spiritual practice, a path toward deeper fulfillment.

Signs of spiritual love:

• Arises in the absence of fear and insecurity.

• It gives without expecting a return.

• Brings peace instead of attachment and turmoil.

Becoming Love Itself

Love, in its most pristine form, is not something we do-it is something we become. When we stopped seeing love from an outer source, adopting it as our natural state made Ananda a simple given.

To dwell in love is to dwell in the imminence of the universe itself. And, in that imminence, we find out that Ananda was not in another person; it was all along within us.

SIXTEEN

SUFFERING AS A GATEWAY – THE UNLIKELY PATHWAY TO DEEP JOY

Suffering is part of life, and no one can escape it. From whining about trivial disappointments to mourning real tragedies, suffering has visited all of us sometime. Can one then dare to suggest that suffering may not be merely an obstruction to happiness but a doorway to Ananda? Indian philosophy teaches that suffering, properly understood, is not an enemy, for it is a teacher-force that can destroy illusions, deepen wisdom, and ultimately fulfill us in all time.

The Misconception of Suffering as Punishment

Most people consider suffering to be some external power against them—an unfair punishment, detestable karma, or just bad luck. But suffering is something that comes down onto us; it is also something that happens for us, refining us and polishing us in ways we rarely see while we are caught in the moment.

According to the Bhagavad Gita, suffering is an indispensable part of the journey toward self-realization. Krishna never promised Arjuna a life without suffering; on the contrary, he taught him to utilize suffering as a means of growth and wisdom instead of as a reason for despair.

Perhaps a stronger question to ask would be, "What is all this teaching me?" rather than "Why is this happening to me?"

Tapa: The Fire of Transformation

In Indian philosophy, Tapa (which literally means "heat") is the transformative power arising from troubles. Just as the fire refines gold by burning away impurities, so too may suffering refine the soul, excising false personas, grasping attachments, and blinding illusions.

The essential things in Tapa are not passive endurance and self-inflicted pain. It is about letting difficulties further shape one's life insight. It teaches three important lessons:

1. **Impermanence** – Nothing lasts forever, not even suffering. Getting this recognition will lessen attachments to both pleasure and pain.

2. **Detachment** – In the face of loss, we realize everything outside is temporary, and temporary encourages us to look inward for stability.

3. **Resilience** - The more we become conscious and aware in addressing suffering, the stronger becomes our inner foundation.

Suffering, once procured with wisdom, doesn't kill; it purifies. Suffering expunges what is false and reveals what is true.

Pain and Suffering as Potentials for Awakening

Almost every spiritual tradition acknowledges that the intervention of pain must wake people up. When life gets too comfy, we drift through it, seldom taking an interest in deeper truths. But when something dreadful occurs to stun us—a breakup happens, our career falls apart, or illness strikes—that suffering stops us in our track and forces us to reflect.

Pain breaks illusions. It shows you what truly matters. It reveals where your attachments lie, where you've been out of alignment, and where greater growth is necessary.

In the Upanishads, suffering is compared to a thunderclap waking up one's soul. Without it, we may never embark on the inward journey. Rather than seeing pain as something to resist, Indian wisdom invites us to see pain as initiation—an invitation to transcend shallow joys into deeper realms.

Moving with Awareness Through Suffering

From the standpoint of achieving deep joy, the conscious navigation of suffering must be one that neither suppresses pain nor becomes overwhelming within it, but rather uses it as a stepping stone. Here are practical steps for that:

1. Accept Fully and Relentlessly

Suffering deepens when we put up a fight. The initial step is radical acceptance—not resignation, but embracing reality for what it is. As soon as we quit fighting with what is, suffering will start to loosen its grip on us.

• Instead of, "This should never have happened!" say, "This is happening—now what?"

· Cognize that pain is a catalyst for growth and not its interruption.

2. Shift from Victim to Learner

The human mind tends to want to find someone or something to blame when it suffers. But blaming keeps one stuck, and it is this shift away from victim to learning that is vital.

· "What is this experience teaching me?" is a question to consider. Every pain contains a lesson.

· Redirect from loss to methods this experience expanded your consciousness.

3. Transmute Pain into Compassion

If we allow it, suffering can pull us into compassion. It grants our first-hand experience of what others go through when they suffer.

· Use your suffering instead of using it to disconnect.

· Remember: Every person has hidden struggles.

· Use your individual pain as a bridge to relate to and help others.

4. Seal Your Detachment from This Illusion of Permanence

From the attachment to the people, things, personality, or even results spring all suffering. The more we hold the opinion that something is important to our state of happiness, the more suffering we go through in losing it.

· Get into a regular habit of talking to yourself: "This too shall pass."

· Know whatever is outside is temporary, whereas your inside self is eternal and unchanging.

Ananda Through Suffering: The Rebirth of the Self

From a paradoxical stand, how can joy come forth from suffering? Yet, the one thing that those who tread the path of self-actualization know to be true.

• In the moment of maximum affliction shall fall the most profound insights.

• The lowest ebb of joy is often touched after the lowest ebb of sorrow.

• Dearth brings freedom from attachment.

Suffering does not bar Ananda; it clears the way for it. It dissolves what is false, breaks the ego, and forces the mind to surrender. And it is in that surrendering, that breaking, that something greater is revealed: the joy that is independent of external conditions.

Gifts of Suffering and the Hidden Rebirth of the Self

Suffering does not just shape character; it reveals our deepest truths. When we stop resisting pain, we begin to see the hidden gifts it carries:

1. **Suffering as a Catalyst for Inner Strength**

• Hardship strengthens resolve. What once seemed unbearable becomes a stepping stone toward resilience.

• Emotional pain forces us to expand beyond our perceived limitations.

• Challenges teach us adaptability—an essential trait for navigating the ever-changing world.

2. **The Most Beautiful Gift of Perspective**

• Stripped to the barest fundamentals, one must see into the very issues that matter.

• The temporary severing of some bonds reminds us most that everything is impermanent, thus we appreciate life all the more.

• Suffering teaches humility as it removes pride and opens one's spirit to wisdom.

3. **Pain Becomes the Rebirth of Oneself**

• When Indian mystics talk about suffering, it is usually in terms of a new birth into spirituality.

· Just as breaking the shell of a seed is necessary for it to become a tree, suffering loosens the stranglehold of the ego, paving the way for the true self to emerge.

· Suffering needs complete surrender on our part; then we stop clinging to the old identities and open ourselves to transformation.

Walking Through Fire to Find the Light

Suffering is not an opponent; rather, it is a mentor, a guide hence a step necessary to Ananda.

Thus, instead of resisting suffering, one is encouraged to embrace it in the unfolding of life. Suffering softens, refines, and deepens one's awareness. When fear disappears from the experience of suffering, nothing remains except wisdom, strength, and unswayable joy always hidden in the nooks of one's self.

Epilogue: Returning To Yourself

Why Ananda Was Never Lost—Only Forgotten

In the enormous spiritual heritage of India, happiness was never regarded as something to pursue—it was considered something to uncover. Ananda, the purest form of bliss, is not a gift for our efforts in the external world but is also not exactly an ephemeral emotion conditioned on circumstances. Rather, it is a natural state of being, an intrinsic part of our true self (Atman): That it was not to be earned, taught really did persuade ancient sages; it needed just to be remembered.

So, why is it so far from modern living? Why must we strive, suffer, and search in vain for fulfillment? It is because, as Indian philosophy has long since warned, avidya (ignorance) and Moha (delusion). We believe happiness is not our very own, pursuable, or available in the possession of something, the achievement of something, or somebody else in doing so, we forget what the Upanishads, the Bhagavad Gita and many such spiritual traditions taught very clearly: That lasting contentment is not an object, but a state of being.

In fact, these modern conditions have made us feel that satisfaction means more of everything (most often money, success, or experiences). But Indian thought says the opposite. True happiness is attained not through bhoga but through tyaga and Santosha. We must only stay detached from the illusion that well-being is in the material world: "He who has no attachment, who neither rejoices nor grieves on obtaining what is good or bad, his wisdom is fixed," says the Bhagavad Gita. This is the essence of Ananda: an unshakable joy that does not rise and fall with life's circumstances.

Ananda seems lost in the illusions that we have created and added to it in the time course, the false identities, desires, fears, and attachments that we keep harboring in our lives. In fact, the Taittiriya Upanishad explains five layers (koshas) involved in human existence, with the innermost being Ananda maya Kosha, the sheath of bliss. This indicates that Ananda is within us but hidden due to these external coverings. The rediscovery path involves not acquiring but peeling off these layers—by questioning what we indeed want, quietening the mind, finding silence.

The sages of India did not give one path to Ananda, for they were aware that the journey differed for everyone. Some may find it via the introspection offered through jnana yoga (the path of wisdom), others through the devotion of bhakti yoga, selfless action in karma yoga, or discipline of raja yoga. All trails lead to liberation from suffering-a being in which happiness is not searched for, because happiness is one with it.

Different ways through the ages have spoken of this. "Brahman alone is real, the world is illusion, and the individual self is none other than Brahman," said Adi Shankaracharya. He pointed in that direction to this truth. When Buddha stated that attachment leads to suffering and non-attachment ends it, he impresses the same truth to the people. When Kabir sang, "Where do you seek me, O devotee? I am neither in temple nor mosque-I am within you," he guided us back to the same realization.

Ananda was never lost. Ananda is only lost. Given that we have allowed outside noise to drown out the silence within. Silence itself has not ceased to be; it still awaits our return. Through these teachings, this book has surveyed the wisdom once foundational in Indian life, but it has not been enough to understand it intellectually. Living it is the only way to claim back Ananda. Simplicity instead of overabundance; presence instead of constant distraction, and a content mind rather than endless seeking.

In not saying that Ananda is not very distant from heaven, it only means that it is buried under layers of forgetfulness. It is the stillness behind every thought, the peace behind every desire, the joy that remains when all else fades. Bliss is not what one wanders about searching for; one is a traveler who has temporarily lost a way home. But the path home is illuminated, as it always has been. All we need to do is remember.

Living This Philosophy Beyond This Book

"A traveler once came to a wise sage in the Himalayas, tired from long wandering in search of fulfillment. 'I have traveled through lands, studied scriptures, meditated in caves,' he said, 'yet peace eludes me still. Tell me, where is true contentment?'

Then the sage smiled and handed him a small lamp. 'This flame,' he said, 'has been burning even before you arrived. If you carry it with care, it will always show you the way'. The traveler takes the lamp, but strong winds blow it off when he is coming down the hill. So, he runs back, agitated. 'Master, the flame is gone!'

The sage laughs. 'No, my child, the flame is not gone-you have simply forgotten how to light it again.'

This is the essence of the wisdom you have encountered in this book. Ananda is like that eternal flame-it never dies; only in the tumult of life do we forget how we attend to it.

The lost teachings of India are not merely intended for read; they are instead to be lived, kindled and protected against the storms of distraction, attachment, and endless striving.

<u>Walking the Path, Not Just Knowing It</u>

Most read intelligence, but very few allow it to transform them into something else. This is because the conditioned mind, although from years of external seeking, resists stillness. Moreover, even though one's understanding is quite clear that joy is found within, it still pulls one outward. This is why real Ananda is not found in knowledge alone but in the true practice-sadhana.

To live this philosophy is to try to change the very way we view our lives. Turning away from sufficient bhoga (pleasure-seeking) to yoga (union with the self), moving away from ichha (desire) toward Santosha (contentment), changing from endless grasping to graceful acceptance-these profound changes require practice, not a one-time realization, and such practice must become a way of life, interwoven with the days of our lives.

Easily, we fall back into old patterns! We measure our worth by performance; we tend to equate happiness with success outside; yet ancient wisdom tells us that real contentment has nothing to do with what we have. It is more about how we perceive what we have. The Yoga Vasistha says: "The mind alone is the cause of bondage and liberation." If we were to train our minds to seek Ananda in simplicity, in the present moment, in connection rather than possession, then fulfillment would no longer be a goal, but, instead, a state of being.

<u>Everyday Ananda Living</u>

How do we embrace this philosophy in the modern world? How do we carry the torch of Ananda amidst responsibility, relationship, and the chaos of daily living?

1. Cultivate Stillness-Surely, the world is loud, but silence is always beneath it. Enters from meditation, mindful breathing, walks, or perhaps just a few moments

to find the inner silence. The Upanishads call this Antar Mouna-that is, the inner silence-where true wisdom is really heard.

2. Detach but engage-Detachment does not mean to withdraw; it means participation without obsession. Nishkama karma, to the Bhagavad Gita, is doing one's duty with full dedication but not being attached to outcome. Do your work, love unconditionally, give generously-but don't chain your happiness to the outcomes.

3. Seek Fulfillment in Being as Opposed to Accumulating-Modern culture sees success as accumulation but Indian philosophy asks us to seek wealth in experience, in presence, in self-consciousness. Contentment (Santosha) is a decision, not a result.

4. Return to the Body and Breath-Ancient teachings say that the body is the temple while breath connects the mind and soul. Simple acts-yoga, mindful eating, and conscious movement-align us to the natural flow of life.

5. Serve Without Desire for Reward-Deep fulfillment erupts when we dissolve the ego into serving others. Random acts of kindness with no expected payback purify the heart and put us in the current of universal joy.

The Journey Never Closes

Heavenly bliss is not the final destination. It is not something we "achieve" and then hold forever. The flame must be kept lit across time by sheer effort, awareness, wisdom, and practice.

As you make the last few turns of this book, carry the following thought into your heart: Your feet have barely begun upon this path. You have walked merely from signpost to signpost among the words you have read, which point to something that has always been within you. The true journey begins now, not in the discovery of something but in the reclaiming of that which was never lost.

And when the winds of life try to blow out your flame, simply smile because now you know how to light it again.

Appendix

<u>**Lessons Summarized: A Guide to Daily Practice**</u>

To understand Ananda is only the beginning; to live it is the real journey. Ancient Indian wisdom was never meant to be relegated to scripture or philosophical discussions; it was supposed to be practiced, embodied in the rhythms and cycles of daily life. The great masters never taught fulfillment as an idea to be philosophically pondered; rather, it was to be an experienced reality woven into the very fabric of action, thought, and breath.

The following lessons are not fixed rules, but gentle invitations urging you not toward something new, but back to what has always been yours. They beckon you to shift your own awareness, perhaps to peer out through different lenses, and to rediscover the joy that has always existed beneath the clamor of the mind.

---

1. Shift from Seeking to Remembering

In the commonly held belief among us, happiness is excessively far into the future, somewhere to be paid for through our efforts, successes, or suitable circumstances. Philosophically, however, Indian tradition teaches us that real fulfillment-Ananda-is not something to be acquired; it is rather something to be uncovered.

Thus, at least each morning for a while, before the demands of the day take over, sit quietly and remind yourself:

"Fulfillment is not in the future; it is already present within me."

This simple shift in thought transforms everything. It liberates the mind from an endless chase and grounds it to the complete here and now. It is an act of recognition whereby not making effort becomes the route toward fulfillment.

---

2. Practice Nishkama Karma - Action Without Attachment

The value we give to our actions depends a lot upon the outcome. Success brings joy; failure brings pain. But the Bhagavad Gita presents a radical alternative: Nishkama Karma-acting with full effort yet without clinging to the result.

Let this principle characterize your life:

• Work honestly and earn your bread but do not attach your joy to that of being praised or recognized.

• Love truly but do not expect anything in return.

• Do your best but do not stake your self-worth on failure.

For Krishna tells Arjuna:

"You have the right to your actions, but never to the fruits of those actions."

The secret is that as soon as you stop needing a specific result, things flow more effortlessly. You no longer function from anxiety but joy.

---

3. Cultivate Santosha-The Art of Contentment

Modern life conditions us to believe that there must be more and, therefore, more is always better-more money, more success, more experiences. Santosha or contentment stands in stark contrast to this insatiable striving. It does not mean settling for what is less; it means getting an understanding that nothing external can complete you.

Each day, stop for a moment and ask yourself, "Do I truly lack something or have I simply forgotten to appreciate what is already here?"

Gratitude is the simplest and most extremely pleasing way to grow in contentment. Instead of hunting down new joys, begin recognizing those already around you: from a single courtesy to the warming sun, from the silence of early morning to the evening sky full of stars.

---

4. Silence the Noise, Listen to the Self

The mind is like an agitated ocean-full of thoughts, worries, and desires. But beneath its choppy surface lies a stillness. The sages of India taught that wisdom does not arise amid noise; it emerges in silence.

So, carve out times for silence in your day:

· In the morning, sit in silence before touching your phone.

· Breathe deeply and consciously when your mind feels agitated.

· Be alone by simply sitting in silence for five minutes.

The Upanishads tell us that whatever answer we are looking for is not anywhere outside; it is inside us. The more we listen in, the more we become conscious of the Ananda which was always there.

---

5. Detach Without Withdrawing

Detachment does not imply withdrawal from the world; it means living fully but remaining unbound. Love deeply. Be engaged fully. Experience life to its fullest and learn not to cling.

Detachment signifies a state of freedom wherein one can enjoy life without being enslaved by it. It is loving someone fully and not allowing their actions to interfere with your peace. It is working busily and not allowing accomplishments and failures to assign worth to you.

Detachment does not equate with indifference; rather, it implies engagement without possessiveness.

6. Find Joy in Simplicity

The mind is always yearning for grand experiences, but Ananda is usually found in the simple moments: a sip of tea, a shared laugh, and the smell of earth after rain.

The ancient sages did not pursue happiness in rare, extraordinary events-but rather in the flow of daily life. Train your mind to notice these moments:

· Feel the texture of your food while you eat instead of rushing through your meal.

· Actually, listen to a person while they speak, as opposed to waiting for your turn to talk.

· Notice the sunset with its changing colors.

As long as we keep looking beyond life, we will not create room for seeing life itself.

7. Align with Dharma-Live with Purpose, Not Pressure

Dharma is not meant by rigid duty; it is about living in tune with one's true nature. Instead of asking, what should I achieve? ask, how can I contribute?

Living in dharma shifts effort away from self-centered ambition toward meaningful action. And life turns from a burden to an expression of joy when work is in true expression to one's inner life.

8. Convert Suffering into Growth

Pain is inevitable; suffering is optional. Hidden beneath scars, every challenge, every loss, every struggle comes with a lesson. Rather than resisting discomfort, ask:

"What is this teaching me?"

According to Bhagavad Gita, pain cannot be worthless if it has made you wiser, and the deepest joy sprouts most of the time from strength earned through pain.

<u>Turn Pain into Growth</u>

Although pain is inevitable, suffering is actually a choice. Every loss or every occurrence of struggle hides a lesson in it. Do not be afraid but ask instead, "What is this really teaching me?" The beauty of the Bhagavad Gita is this: there is no such thing as needless pain, as all pain contributes to deeper wisdom. The broadest joy usually comes from the psychological walls erected by calamities.

---

9. Breathe, Be Present, Let Go

Come back, really, to this moment, and it's as simple and profound as that.

- A deep breath now.
- Your feet on the ground.
- Mind the rise and fall of your chest.

The past is history; the future is mystery; only in the present is Ananda.

---

10. Remember: Ananda Never Went Away

Remember to come back to this every day:

I am never separate from fullness; I am fullness itself.

Beneath layers of conditioning, of desires and fears, rests that still, unshaken joy always waiting to be remembered. It is not becoming someone else; it is about seeing who you always were.

Not merely in words but in rising, working, loving, and letting go, let this philosophy be.

Ananda was never lost; it has been waiting for you all along.

Recommended Readings For Deeper Exploration

Notes

<u>**A Guide to Daily Practice**</u>

In the quest for Ananda, or true fulfillment, we often get caught up in the whirlwind of life, attempting to achieve certain goals that promise us some happiness, only to end in a greater void. With profound insights into the mind and the nature of happiness, Indian philosophy offers the deeper path—a path that does not encourage us to search for happiness in far-off destinations or unreachable goals but rather in the very fabric of everyday life. True fulfillment, Ananda, cannot be attained; it can only be awakened. It lies, therefore, in being completely aware of the fullness of life, that every moment holds the prospect of joy and peace.

From these notes, we distill the wisdom of the Indian tradition as you go about fulfilling yourself through simple yet deep practices that build presence, awareness, and meaning into each day. These are not stiff routines or formulas for an easy happiness but an invitation to embrace life as it is; to unlock yourself to the subtle joys and truths that permeate every moment of your existence.

1. Presence: The Art of Awakening to the Moment

Possibly the greatest gift in Indian philosophy is encouraging us to be present. Forever being thrust into the future; we lose sight of this wonderful gift given by the present moment. The Bhagavad Gita holds that peace is found in living in the present, rather than being attached to our past or striving for a future that may never come. There is no Ananda in the past or the future; the present is only accessible upon stopping, paying attention, and getting immersed in the events occurring around us.

To recognize presence is beginning to recognize life through the examination of every sacred minute before us, wherein each minute presents an opportunity for experience-lifting joy, peace, and clarity. It is the conscious choice to disengage from automatic machinery and to become aware of life around us, distinguishing it from the profane. In stillness or while listening to another, each moment entrusts us with the power to reconnect with our inner peace and live Ananda.

2. **Santosha: The Freedom Found in Contentment**

Indian philosophy observes the practice of Santosha, or contentment. We live in a world where the ever-increasing desire for more—more material possessions, more achievements, more recognition—leads our thinking to believe that happiness is something to be gained or attained. But ancient wisdom implies otherwise: happiness is not something that comes from outside but an inner state of being that arises when we learn to be content with what is.

Contentment does not mean that you are settling for less or are giving up on a life that lacks luster. This state of being sees much more abundance here and within us. As we shift our focus from what is lacking to what already is, we become enveloped in deep inner joy and serenity regardless of external conditions. This practice of Santosha invites us to trust what is, recognize we are enough as we are, and know that true fulfillment comes not from hoarding but rather from surrendering to, accepting, and giving thanks for what is.

3. **Karma-Yoga: Living Purpose-Filled in Every Act**

Karma Yoga, the path of unselfish action, elucidates that every endeavor, large or small, can become a means to deliverance. For this to happen, the doing of the action needs to be done without attachment to its results, offered to God. With this attitude in surrender and service, we transcend the ego-centered pursuit of success and experience harmony in action.

Do not forget the sacredness of the act: that is what Indian philosophy teaches. The action itself, and its intention with presence, became what is priceless. By treating every action as a service, we make every deed—whether caring for one, working for pay, or even washing dishes—an act of our own respect. This practice frees us from the worry of results and enables us to enjoy the acts themselves.

4. Vairagya: The Art of Detachment

Detachment is referred to as Vairagya—not detachment from life, but from the attachment to results, desires, and fleeting approval. The lightness with which one holds the world is the very virtue of participating in it fully without being entrapped by it. Such detachment has never meant indifference, mockery, or withdrawal from an entity; it is rather to accept the transient nature of all things and to find peace therein.

With detachment, we learn to let go of rigid expectations and judgments of how things should be. Once we relinquish the demand for control and perfection, we open ourselves to life as it flows naturally, free without hindrance. This openness cultivates an inner sanctuary, and from within that space, it dawns that joy is never to be gotten; rather, it is awakened when we cease striving against life's inherent unpredictability.

5. Self-Inquiry: Path to True Knowing

In Indian philosophical thought, the practice of self-inquiry is considered one of the strongest tools for inner transformation. It stands as the art of turning one's mind inwards, questioning oneself deeply through what we are, what we truly wish for, and what is actually submerged beneath the surface of thought and desire. This mental journey unearths our illusions of perception and enables us to touch base with the deeper truths of our being.

Self-inquiry does not entail going around looking outside for answers; it has to do with exploring internally for answers that have always been there. In this inner marketplace, the realization dawns that Ananda is not found in external situations but is realized within our true nature. It is, for sure, a bumpy pathway but one that does lead to unclouded clear vision, and soothing stillness emerges from there as we discard the layers of conditioning and ego that hungrily guard the lamplight within.

6. Interconnectedness: Finding Joy in Unity

Indian thought lays great emphasis on the interconnectedness of all beings, on the divine thread that runs through everything. When we understand our own unique place in this web of life, we can delight in the wellness of others as well as our own. Ananda expands, and as we connect with our surroundings, we realize that happiness for one is happiness for all. In this perspective, we grow to recognize the divine in every human, every animal, every plant, and every part of nature. This consciousness changes the way we relate and interact with the world, bringing a sense of unity and peace that transcend personal wants and separateness.

Non-attachment: the path of freedom in surrender

Non-attachment, as defined by Indian philosophy, has nothing to do with denouncing the pleasures or responsibilities of human life; rather, it has everything to do with letting go of control and possessiveness. Non-attachment allows for the full-fledged experience of life while keeping oneself free from emotional and mental entanglements. It invites us to respond with equanimity to the alternating nature of life, realizing the transience of all-not only the good but the evil as well.

Thus, non-attachment stands for living life in its fullness without being trapped by it. This means that we enjoy the beauty of relationships, accomplishments, and pleasures without attachment. This freedom is what leads to peace, and within that peace, we find Ananda.

Living the Wisdom of India's Lost Philosophy

The teachings presented here are not a collection of guidelines to be followed; they are an invitation to live consciously, with presence and compassion. They invite us to turn our gaze inward, where we can shift our focus from the external to the internal and from the transient to the eternal. Much wisdom from Indian philosophy shows us how to recognize and accept Ananda, not to seek it, in every moment.

Remember, on the road of its fulfillment, when we live in harmony with our true nature, when we have engaged life with an open heart, and when we let each moment be as it is, that is when the true joy arises. The lost philosophies of India provide an ageless road map to Ananda; a journey that beckons you to uncover great joy hidden in the mundane.